D1541711

Who the Hell Told You That?

An Eviction Notice for Indoctrinated Thoughts

Dr. Melissa Carver

Foreword by Davidji

WHO THE HELL TOLD YOU THAT?: AN EVICTION NOTICE FOR INDOCTRINATED THOUGHTS

Copyright © 2020 Dr. Melissa Carver

Artwork by Inked up Ari

1405 SW 6th Avenue • Ocala, Florida 34471 • Phone 352-622-1825 • Fax 352-622-1875
Website: www.atlantic-pub.com • Email: sales@atlantic-pub.com
SAN Number: 268-1250

No part of this publication may be reproduced, stored in a retrieval system, or transmitted in any form or by any means, electronic, mechanical, photocopying, recording, scanning, or otherwise, except as permitted under Section 107 or 108 of the 1976 United States Copyright Act, without the prior written permission of the Publisher. Requests to the Publisher for permission should be sent to Atlantic Publishing Group, Inc., 1405 SW 6th Avenue, Ocala, Florida 34471.

Library of Congress Control Number: 2020912379

LIMIT OF LIABILITY/DISCLAIMER OF WARRANTY: The publisher and the author make no representations or warranties with respect to the accuracy or completeness of the contents of this work and specifically disclaim all warranties, including without limitation warranties of fitness for a particular purpose. No warranty may be created or extended by sales or promotional materials. The advice and strategies contained herein may not be suitable for every situation. This work is sold with the understanding that the publisher is not engaged in rendering legal, accounting, or other professional services. If professional assistance is required, the services of a competent professional should be sought. Neither the publisher nor the author shall be liable for damages arising herefrom. The fact that an organization or Web site is referred to in this work as a citation and/or a potential source of further information does not mean that the author or the publisher endorses the information the organization or Web site may provide or recommendations it may make. Further, readers should be aware that Internet Web sites listed in this work may have changed or disappeared between when this work was written and when it is read.

TRADEMARK DISCLAIMER: All trademarks, trade names, or logos mentioned or used are the property of their respective owners and are used only to directly describe the products being provided. Every effort has been made to properly capitalize, punctuate, identify, and attribute trademarks and trade names to their respective owners, including the use of ® and ™ wherever possible and practical. Atlantic Publishing Group, Inc. is not a partner, affiliate, or licensee with the holders of said trademarks.

Printed in the United States

PROJECT MANAGER: Kassandra White

Acknowledgments

Wow! I am surrounded by badasses who encourage my badassery. For years my husband and children have been along for the ride, always down for my crazy adventures and encouraging my success, whatever that may look like to me. From staying up too late talking about all the new research I discovered or being mindful of when it's time to just let me be locked in my office without interruption, truly, these humans that are within my family unit are my rock, my nurturers, and my voices of love. Leo, Amir, Asiya, and Aaron, there are no words that properly express my gratitude.

My friend Shelly Hallock, you have attended almost every single event that I have ever facilitated. Your love and unconditional determination to be in my front row has meant the world to me.

Thank you to my lifelong friend, Shannon Cooper. You have done nothing but cheer me on since 7th grade! I cannot imagine my life without you in it. So many memories!! Thank you for also being the very first to read this book before its release. I couldn't wait until publication to share yet another life milestone with you.

To my teacher, mentor, and friend, Davidji, never in life did I have a mentor until you. From the very first time I sat in a room with over four hundred other people as we all listened to your teachings, I knew we would be friends. What intuition didn't tell me was just how much you were going to help me, influence me, guide me, encourage me, and make time for me even when you were traveling the world. #MyFrontRow

Megan Monahan and Shelly Tygielski, I admire you both so much. Your missions and your voices inspire so many. Thank you for your advice and friendship.

To my mom, Wanda, thank you for all of your words of encouragement and always believing in me. Most importantly, thank you for your willingness to begin the self-knowledge journey, so that you may heal, we may heal. "Every woman who heals herself helps heal all the women who came before her, and all those who come after her." ~ Christiane Northrup.

To each of you who have supported me in various ways, you are appreciated. Stephanie Head, Sheryl Richardson, Ariana Shelton, Teresa Johnson, Amanda Mills, Gayle Branson, Bridgett Craig, Rita Alkasrany, Judy Brock, Bessie Harts, Wendell Harts, Dawn Peak, Mike Hafiz, Dwarn Carver, Lee Carver, Damaris Murphy, Danielle Carver, Quesa VanWinkle, Gail Combs, and Amber Freeman.

I love each of you listed above with my whole soul!

Table of Contents

Foreword

You were born whole & perfect & pure — fully aligned with the flow of the universe. For nine months — as you comfortably rested in the womb — you listened to the primal drum beat of your mother's heart synchronizing you with the stars, the phases of the moon, the rhythm of the seasons, and the rising & setting of the sun. All of your needs were effortlessly met — you received nourishment from a tube that flowed oxygenated blood & nutrients directly into your body, and — magically — everything not essential to your development & growth was seamlessly released back out. It was a sweet set-up. And then, on that auspicious day of your birth, you graced the world with your presence. But, that was also the defining moment when you became aware that all of your needs were no longer being met automatically.

Suddenly, your comfort, nourishment, and the fulfillment of your basic needs of the heart - attention, affection, appreciation, and acceptance - were in the hands of someone else. In those early years, where your language skills were unevolved, you would smile, pout, cry, or giggle to summon your caretaker and receive the fulfillment you desired in the moment. And, over time, you reinforced these behaviors to satisfy your every wish — programming others in the most effective way — as you subliminally programmed yourself.

As you moved into your childhood and adolescence, your formal conditioning of life began. The brilliant author Don Miguel Ruiz refers to this process as domestication — where you learn to navigate the world around you through an infinite unfolding of choices followed by corresponding punishments and rewards. Our sense of what's right-and-wrong... what's acceptable behavior and what's not... the crafting of our personality... and even the development of our belief systems all come from this series of life experiences presenting themselves to us, and based on what's worked in the past, we progressively tame ourselves.

Over time, we begin to make choices that are out of alignment in order to experience what we think will bring us more happiness, more gratification, more "success", and more ease; we make decisions that contradict what we feel inside in order to experience less sadness, less loneliness, less pain, and less "failure." We compromise the wholeness that was the starting point for our life's journey. And in our quest to receive the acceptance of our friends, the admiration of our peers, the "likes" of those on social media, and the approval of society, we start to behave in ways that are out of alignment with who we really are.

The consequences can be devastating. The truest and most valid aspects of our self become hidden; we dim our light in moments where it needs to shine; we play small, and our voice weakens; our creativity & potential for growth withers; and in the process, we end up sacrificing our authenticity... our integrity... our purpose in life... the true reason for us being here... to love more & to be happy.

How do we return to the memory of our wholeness? How do we learn to let love in again? How do we step back into our power? How do we re-kindle the fire that once burned within us?

These are deep questions — but do not despair — because there actually is a way back to our most authentic self... to the alignment we all seek... to powerful manifestation & magnificent self-actualization. And, Dr. Melissa Carver is the ideal guide to help you on *your* journey into self-healing & personal transformation. She is the perfect fusion of ancient teachings and real-world practical application. I know her heart. I know her story. I know the results she has achieved in boldly making peace with her past. And, I know how fiercely she has stepped into her power to shine her magnificence. She is a warrior of truth and light. And, I am honored to call her my friend.

For more than a decade, Dr. Carver studied with me in my capacity as the dean of Chopra Center University — ultimately mastering the timeless wisdom of meditation & mindbody healing. She then cultivated her own signature process to shatter the limiting beliefs that hold each of us back from living our dream life.

In the following pages, she candidly shares her own story of returning to wholeness... revealing the secrets that so many people at the crossroads have used to take their lives to the next level, and she guides you on a powerful journey back to your most genuine self. You will instantly connect with her heart-felt, authentic voice and realize that she is speaking directly to *your* heart. *Who the Hell Told You That?* unfolds like an owner's manual to life brimming with profound wisdom, deep reflections, and practical action steps to help you let go of the past, embrace your truth, and step into your power. Each chapter will move you closer to clarity as you awaken a deeper understanding of who you are, a confidence in where you need to go, and the courage to own your impact. You will finish the book with a renewed sense of self, daily affirmations to help you keep raising your vibration, a personalized blueprint to move through your greatest constrictions, and high-velocity inspiration to live your best life. Dr. Carver will lovingly and gracefully take you to that place of life-affirming rebirth — and all you need to do once you're there... is to lean hard in the direction of your dreams & desires.

So, let your journey to wholeness begin!

—davidji, author of Sacred Powers

Introduction

Whose thoughts do we hear during those conversations with self? What triggers our motivation, fear, love, ambition, and peace? Throughout the navigation of life's challenges, we rely on one or a combination of the following; subconscious, intuition, analysis, logic, or the unconscious. When these tools are compartmentalized, only one is outside the realm of the daily life we have lived.

Perspectives are unique to each of us. You and I have lived different lives, but even if we had not, your context and feelings about that life would still not be completely parallel with mine. You may have heard of siblings, twins even, who grew up in the same household and attended the same school and who have grown into two completely different people. Each of us processes the information that life gives us very differently. We collect this information and use it as the data for what we want or don't want in life.

Until we stop to analyze these downloads of information, we may be completely unaware of the negative aspects that we have held onto. Sometimes even "positive programming" can interrupt our personal progress.

I grew up fighting so hard against external programming that I created my own form of inhibition. That's the thing with our subconscious... it tries hard to protect, not necessarily grow. It took me some time to realize that I, the free thinker, the rebel against all forms of boxed thinking, had too fallen victim. Since I'm not a fan of allowing anything to victimize me for long, the journey of self-knowledge became one of my most important missions.

It is my deepest intention to help you see new perspectives. Utilizing these new views of you and the world to unlock genuine joy, manifesting desires, and love of yourself in pure form.

I'm not claiming to have all the answers, but I may just have some new questions...

"The privilege of a lifetime is to become who you truly are."

—C.G. JUNG

CHAPTER 1

Naked Truth

To fit in means you will never stand out. It's the safe game. The job of fitting in seems to really hit hard during those middle and high school years. Many of us try to figure out who we are while simultaneously wanting to fit in, have friends, and be liked. It is human nature to want a tribe, a group going through similar circumstances with whom we can share our thoughts and feelings. But where do we draw a line when it comes to our own authenticity? For many people, this line gets thinner over time. Transitioning from adolescence into adulthood can go from very little responsibility to bills and overload rather quickly. This transition leaves little space for free, unbridled self-discovery. As we move forward in the constraints of obligation most of us feel like it doesn't really matter who we are. Is the rent paid and baby fed? Are the dishes done? It's unfortunate that so many people feel the anxiety and stresses of adulthood before they allow themselves a proper time span to explore their likes and dislikes, but it's never too late. Priorities change as we grow as well, and the experiences you encountered were to place you exactly where you are. If you feel as though there were areas of yourself that you did not allow a majority to see, then some of your personal lessons involve exploring that.

Once a taste of fitting in has hit the palate, it can become addicting. The thoughts of saying or doing something outside of your normal routine may make you question what your friends and family will think. For example, if you're someone who has always worn designer clothes but now your views or style have changed, you may wonder what your circle will think if you buy your next outfit from Goodwill. A little more extreme than clothing may be political views, the sexual orientation of who you now find attractive, or how you shift your personal stance on what disciplining a child looks like. This was a big one for me. Not only how I disciplined, but also the reasons why or why not. I grew up in an environment where everyone spanked their children. They spoke often about how children in general needed to be spanked more. They also seemed to blame the world problems on this topic. The older generation not only felt more physical discipline was needed for the children, but also felt that it had not been conducted enough on those who were now stepping into adult roles. I remember it being a topic quite often really. Adults discussing how this or that parent needed to whoop their kid. Sometimes it was other parents they knew or other times just a random incident in a store. Although, they usually did not know the details of what was happening or if that parent does or does not spank. Not one time do I remember anyone questioning if the child was okay or if there were mental health issues at play. When my oldest son was around thirteen or fourteen, I had an epiphany. I had spanked him to look like a good parent. This was completely from the subconscious. It came from a desire to be viewed as a mom who was loving but also didn't allow unruliness to go without a "good old-fashioned ass whooping." That's what a lot of the people I was around liked to call a spanking. At this stop on the timeline of my life, I was starting over with two more babies, only thirteen months apart. No longer being a sixteen-year-old mom and having moved far past what others thought of my parenting, I wanted to raise these two differently, no spankings. I was aware of the negative side effects that spanking could potentially have and wanted the ways from previous generations to stop with me.

The bulk of people want to be accepted in something, sometimes in anything. People can become so engulfed in the thought of being a part of something that they lose who they are. It doesn't take long for a person to completely forget their true interests, opinions, in some cases, even heritage. This is easily observed in "troubled teens." More often than not, when a teenager decides to join a gang or involve themselves with people who are getting into unlawful or personal acts of harm, it's not because it's fun. In most cases, it's because they want a family, people to connect with. The street and gang life can feel like the only option by the time they have submitted. The same scenario plays itself out in other cliques but sometimes not as obvious or blatantly problematic. How did you push your personal boundaries, thoughts, and authenticity to fit in as a teen? How much of that thought process carried over as an adult?

Office politics are in every single employment situation. Do you leave work feeling like you transform into who you really are as soon as you exit the building? Do you let a sigh of relief flow out of your body because you can now breathe?

I have a friend who worked for a powerful, wealthy man. She expressed to me that his opinion of women, minorities, and moral standards did not align with her own. She had to hear him degrade individuals on a regular basis, and she opted to bite her tongue. It was a good job with excellent pay and benefits. One can understand why a mother would be reluctant to stand up for people she didn't know or were outside of her household when it could result in losing her income. But how much harm does this do to her?

Working in an environment where we feel like we will lose our job for our personal beliefs or hearing others degrade people that we want to speak up for can take its toll on our spirit and mind. The friend I mentioned above eventually found a new career path, one that aligns with who she is, meeting more people on the mission to help improve the lives of others rather than just degrading them from lack of understanding. This doesn't mean we need to always agree or find people that always agree with us, but placing ourselves in a toxic environment day after day for forty hours or more per week will certainly have side effects. Eventually chipping away at who we are and who we are striving to become.

When on a spiritual path or a mission to become a better human, people often become scared of the idea of always having to be or act positively. If everyone who is living as a yogi, practicing meditation, or has a form of spiritual practice tells you that they are positive all the time, they are not being honest with you or themselves. Being spiritual doesn't mean you're always positive; it means you will trust the universe to find the path through the bullshit. It also means you now have a choice to find the lesson and evolve. I will discuss more on the dangers of being positive all the time a little later on.

If you're honest with yourself, there are one or a few categories that could use your attention when it comes to expressing your true self. Pay close attention to the people or groups you are around when you hold yourself back. Maybe it's an opinion, but also be aware of actions you withhold. Is there one group of friends that you will be silly around but when that side of you attempts to emerge outside of that circle you lasso it back? Maybe they have never seen that side. What would they think? Would it change their perspective of you? Perhaps, but what if it created an even closer friendship with some? Sometimes it becomes so much of a habit to transform based on environment that we tell ourselves, "that's just how the world is," and now we believe our own words. Why wouldn't we?

Most of us have heard that we should compartmentalize our friend groups, work, church, school, sport teams, and so forth until everything we do is broken down into various aspects of ourselves. We did, however, have a different opinion at some point as a child. The faith was there to do better, to live more of life on our terms. After a few obstacles and getting knocked down more than we care to remember, we begin to tell ourselves that our parents were right, and we stop showing most others who we really are. I live in an area that just voted to be "moist." A county over just voted in to be "wet." No, I'm not trying to talk dirty to you. These are real terms pertaining to alcohol sales. Yes, prohibition never ended in multiple counties in Kentucky. If you don't live in one of these geographical locations that also did not or does not yet allow any alcohol sales, you're probably going to need a minute or two to process that. There are several church organizations in this area that do not want to allow people to legally purchase alcohol in their county, but what I am now hearing from some of those church members is the sad fact that they all just lie to each other. I was recently having small talk in a restaurant with a woman who was telling me how much she would love a glass of wine. I said, "Well, now you can have a glass with your dinner." She said, "Oh no! I can't do that here. People who go to my church may see me." This was one conversation of many. The church should be the space where we can feel safe discussing who we are, but I've learned that few people feel that way. There are people in our city who refuse to eat at restaurants that chose to take advantage of the new law, but they will drive thirty minutes out of their way to eat at an out of town restaurant that also serves alcohol, but "they always have or they didn't vote in our city," is what one couple said to me. If they feel this strongly on the matter, you can understand why church brothers and sisters are in fear of being judged. The questions I ask are how many of those same people also drink but hide it? How many of those people do other things that they also hide? This is by no means picking on any church but just an example of how I watch others live inauthentically to appease the ideas of those they know. I worked in a club for many years. I watched Muslims do the exact same thing. They would order water and their alcoholic drink. When another Muslim came in but was not in their close friend group, they drank the water and pretended the alcoholic drink belonged to someone else. While alcohol may not be on the top healthiest drinks list, it can be done in moderation and responsibly. How many of these people are attempting to drink their sadness away that stems from no real connection with other humans? When free to be ourselves, we often stop or slow down our destructive behavior.

Another example, if you work long hours while living paycheck to paycheck, you may have convinced yourself that working all the time is just how life is. I know a woman who worked extremely hard her entire life. She was not a college graduate, never travelled, and honestly just hadn't explored much that life had to offer. She didn't believe a person in her shoes could do better financially, afford vacations, or level up in her company. She lived with an extremely negative husband. He, too, shared her beliefs and worse. When a light of positivity or a dream entered her mind, it was quickly shot down. After several years of this, they divorced. Her life seemed to turn around quickly after the separation. Travelling to exotic locations, earning more money, and feeling happiness were important again. In these types of situations, we have forgotten who our authentic self even is or was. We hear so much antagonism that it begins to sink in, especially after just one experience validates it. Often people feel that those

childhood convictions around goals and dreams were just based upon ig-
norance of how the world "really is." Were they? Or are children so faithful,
so connected to the source that they have no reservations about what they
can accomplish? I hope you choose the latter. Now as adults our mission is
to find our way back to that place of pure assurance and endless potential.
Kind of funny how that works out. Most of us spend our entire childhood
pretending we're adults, looking forward to having endless freedom with
no rules and countless possibilities. All to grow up and find out you have
to learn how to think like a kid again. It reminds me of a comment that
Jim Carrey once said about being in the gap between human and spiritual consciousness, realizing that he was literally everything. He said, "Ever
since that moment I've just been trying to get back there." That is now our
goal as adults, getting back to a connection with the universe so strong that
regardless of how weird, bizarre, or outlandish others may find our ideas we
have no concern about pleasing their conditioned thoughts.

Let's go back to the positivity subject. Being positive all the time is not authentic. It will not manifest solely positive outcomes in your life by holding
back your true feelings about others or situations. As much as I encourage
my clients and students to strive for positivity, I also encourage authenticity. That means at some point they will not be on the good vibes only viewpoint. It's not only impossible to always be cheerful, but it's also unhealthy.

I was nine months pregnant having my regular checkup. The nurse taking
my blood pressure said, "You have the best blood pressure I've ever seen on
someone as far along as you." I responded with, "That's because I cuss people out as I go!" She said, "You know there's a lot of truth to that." I didn't
mean I cussed people out literally every time I got upset, but back then I
didn't have the same anger control methods or mindfulness, so I was a lot
quicker to jump to that reaction than I am today.

People are often surprised to find out that I still have no problem losing my
shit on someone if that's what it takes. Being mindful and thinking about
our reactions doesn't mean we never get pissed off or have emotions that
make us sad or angry. It means that we attempt to stop first, think about
why this is happening and what lessons are there for us, and get ourselves

to an understanding. The more we understand, the less we have reactions over the same topics. This doesn't mean triggers are not real. It also doesn't mean that everyone you come into contact with is always going to be kind. Should we, as people who want to manifest more positive outcomes just allow others to treat us with disrespect? Do we allow everything to roll off our backs, allow physical, and mental abuse? The answer is absolutely not. I personally witnessed what that conditioned thinking turns into. With a physically abusive father and a mother who was raised that you don't get divorced, I've seen it only gets worse. This is not suggesting a person cannot change. However, they have to not only want to change, but also be committed to the work. The person being abused must let them know that this treatment will not be tolerated under any circumstances. You can honor the authenticity of another person from a distance.

Gloria Steinem said, "The truth will set you free, but first it will piss you off." This quote is at the top of my all-time favorites. The more I learned about my Native and Moorish heritage/history, the angrier I became at the school system for not teaching all of us this information. Even more, I was angry at the political structure that betrayed my ancestors and still to this day has not publicly acknowledged the truth. Finally, I realized that my anger toward a system that only knows of my existence through paying taxes was not helpful. However, that initial rage did fuel my fire to teach others both sides of the story. I still sometimes teach children at the Carnegie Center about Moorish History. Would years of spreading this untold story have been part of who I am without anger? No. The frequency of anger can be transformed into productivity and passion.

I know many who have learned of various truths, gotten angry, and stayed there. Staying in anger stunts personal evolution and has its own dangers. The goal of being a positive person is not to be positive all the time; it is to examine the situation and be honest with yourself and with others. While in the process, you can then transform that negative energy into positive action, creating balance and authenticity through honest expressions on both positive and negative.

If a person is always positive, that means they are suppressing some type of negative emotion. Maybe it's because they feel it is weak to allow an outside force to affect them or perhaps, they feel like they don't have time for a good cry. Sometimes negative feelings are withheld from others to avoid confrontation. There are various reasons as to why someone may think positivity at all times is beneficial, but the outcome can be detrimental.

One of two things will happen to unexpressed sadness or anger. Either it will go into various places of the body, or one day something bad happens, and it will all come crashing in at one time. This can lead to depression and searching for unhealthy forms of escape due to the extreme overload of years of suppressed emotions.

"Some research suggests that inappropriately expressing anger — such as keeping anger pent up — can be harmful to your health. Suppressing anger appears to make chronic pain worse while expressing anger reduces pain,"[i] according to the Mayo Clinic.

Expressing anger doesn't always mean that we have to raise our voice or act out of character, either. When we say the word anger, we often think of someone screaming or ready to fight. If we take a moment to ask why we are angry and then have a conversation, we can accomplish clear communication, as well as keep ourselves level headed.

Politics, bullies, child suffering, daily conversation with negative Nancy at the office, an over-packed Walmart. All these things are going to get on your nerves from time to time, trigger anger, or make you sad. It is okay to admit that.

Then we must also face the issue of trauma. When we live in a violent, abusive environment or have faced an experience that caused great suffering, we may subconsciously repress emotions or turn them off to be able to continue throughout life. The longer we do this, the less we are aware of what we are doing. It becomes normal, and we think that we are not affected. "Those who repress their feelings have developed a perceived effective coping skill that may be adequate in the short-term, but is not functional for your health in the long run," says Dr. Reinke

"Yale's medical school researchers have begun to put together a personality portrait of the person prone to being a repressor. Usually, they are the people who are rational and do not exude emotion, care about meeting other people's needs, and are dependable and successful. However, their marriages and close relationships can go poorly because they are unable to emotionally engage in close intimate relationships."[ii] This is, of course, a self-protective reaction. It is not necessarily because they don't want to emotionally connect with another human.

"Stanford researchers believe one in every six people may be a repressor. In a study of 120 managers and engineers at an aerospace company, the researchers found that repressors had higher blood pressure and reacted with an even greater rise in blood pressure to a simple stress test than non-repressors did. Yale's study found that of 312 patients treated at an outpatient clinic, repressors tended to have lower levels of certain disease-fighting cells of the immune system and higher levels of cells that multiply at the time of allergic reactions."[iii]

Those within our family unit can drive us to the point of wanting to explode sometimes, it's kinda their part-time job. The universe sends us those who we will love with our entire soul, but they, too, have upsetting days, and they, too, need to be authentic and tell us when we are out of line. Even though their truth may piss us off, if we express the anger with our words, analyze the anger internally, and then search for the lesson, we come out on the other side thankful that we have those individuals to shake us up. We can then, and only then, be truly grateful, evolved, and positive about the situation.

As you can see, being positive all the time has its downfalls. There can be no light without the darkness. To manifest a more genuine abundance of happiness and health it is crucial that we accept the low moments. When we take the time (yes, it will take time) to work through our triggers mindfully, we can then find the positive outcome with deeper understanding. Thus, those triggers bother us less and less as more discernment comes. The mindfulness practices placed throughout this book will help you create a practice of self-awareness that gradually transforms into a daily lifestyle. Buddha stated, "I bring you great and good news. There is a way from the crushing miseries of this transitory life to real happiness, and it is open to all. But the way is hard, and there is no magical method of making it easy. It means strenuous and constant self-examination." Beginning the practice can certainly feel strenuous. If you are a beginner, you must realize you have an entire lifespan that you will now have realizations about. Not getting too stuck on those or beating yourself up about regrettable choices is fundamental to moving forward. True happiness comes more of who you are after the layers of camouflage we often wear to blend in are stripped away. The next time you see a "Good Vibes Only" sign remember, sometimes that just means getting the current sorrow to the perspective of good. Trust the process.

Being authentic at times may also cost us our "family" and "friends". They may not agree with your choices or lifestyle so strongly that they end communication with you altogether. This is painful, sometimes excruciating. If it is a situation when a parent or child will no longer be in your presence it can feel like grief for someone who you know is still very capable of being in your life. I cannot tell you what to do in this situation, it is a choice for you alone. But by beginning the questions of…

- How much does this person love me versus their "idea" of me?

- Am I okay with receiving shallow/surface level love from others and losing myself in the process?

- How many other people will give me pure, unconditional love if I am honest?

- How many will I inspire by being authentic?

To attract the right people into our lives we must be authentic in who we are. Otherwise we are attracting those who like the false version that we allow the world to see. Love versus lust. Liking a character in a movie versus loving the soul of the actor. Only you can choose what type of relationships you wish to have.

"Learn from yesterday, live for today,
hope for tomorrow.
The important thing is not to
stop questioning."

—ALBERT EINSTEIN

CHAPTER 2

Throwback

Throwback isn't just for Thursday. We have all heard to not look back, we aren't going that way. We are told to let go of the past; it doesn't matter anymore… Or does it? When the same situations and challenges continue to show themselves in our lives, it's because of us, not the other people. The world isn't against us. Something in our thought process and problem-solving ability in that particular category needs to be unlocked.

The real problem is, we only know what we know. We each grew up in a different household with a different set of rules. The ideas of one or two people are what we heard or observed the most. We then process this information and decide if it is for us or not for us. Even then, when conscious of it, did we truly question any options outside those two scenarios? Life moves fast, even as a child. Personal enjoyment, agendas, chores, school, social engagement… very few homes have time set aside for reflection and self-knowledge. At the end of childhood, we have gathered information from all of those in our lives, various genres of entertainment, and experiences, and then created a picture in our mind of what we want our life to look like. When that picture doesn't unfold and we seem to repeat particular negative situations, it's time to stop, reflect, and question what we think and feel about life. We have our surface-level thoughts that we know exist. What about the thoughts we don't know are there? The ones that we think others share because it's all we've ever known?

As I already shared with you, my dad didn't do anything to actively improve our household. No laundry, cleaning, or cooking. Not one memory of him ever in a grocery store. I'm sure he must've gone to a grocery once he and my mom divorced, but I don't remember it. This is turn shaped my mind to go extreme opposite with my perspectives, requirements, and standards for my relationships. I was determined to have a partner who would do all of these things, not just for me, but for us. He must have the perspective that when it needs to be done, the person best suited at that moment would just execute. Looking back I can't deny that when it came to housework I probably even wanted my partner to do more than me in most cases. I was hardcore. Perhaps this was to overcompensate for my own little psychological, unconscious game. I wanted everyone to notice that I did not follow in my mother's footsteps when it came to sex determined roles or being taken advantage of. When I first met my husband, I said something about him going to the store. He said he didn't want to go. Before he could even finish his statement, I completely lost my shit on him. You know the ones. A full-blown temper tantrum! One hundred percent bloop session (you know you've done them too)! Full of aggression! Every negative thought I ever had toward my dad all came crashing down on him. All because of my experience and utter determination to have a partner who believed in equality. After I calmed down, I realized he didn't mean ever or that day even; he meant he didn't want to go at that exact moment. This was one of my many realizations that I had been dispensing outrage on every man who ever sparked a triggering thought about my dad or my personal stance on how I would be respected. Ugghhhh, not good. This was an extremely unhealthy perspective, not only for every man I came in contact with and my children, but also myself.

I had a client who came to me for advice on manifesting more abundance. Because her parents had told her that she should not ask for too much, she also believed this about the universe and manifesting too many blessings back to back. I asked her if she had an unlimited supply of rice would she mind if the same people came to her daily to be gifted the rice? She said, "Of course not!" This was just the point of view she needed to tap into the realization that the universe does not limit our blessings or judge us for asking for another supportive manifestation. Such a simple metaphor proved to be extraordinarily life changing for her.

The universe is an unlimited supply, but we have been taught there is a limit to everything and that things come with a great sacrifice. This view has been the leash on many of those who dream. It is important that we pursue the dream. However, move through the clouds that keep your visions grounded in fantasy.

To hit the bullseye, we must first pull back the arrow. Reflection into our past will decode the thoughts that constrict our growth. Carl Jung states, "The greatest burden a child must bear is the unlived life of its parents." Parents are usually trying to do their very best to raise us. The struggle for all of us arises in the fact that anyone can only act or react from their level of consciousness. Caught up in survival mode, they project their fears, deficient achievements, and negative life experiences onto their children. The negative words that come from adults as we grow are not just said out of personal fear but also the fear of us making the same mistakes they made or witnessed. This can cause detriment. Stating that you must break through what you learned from broken people doesn't mean you love or respect them any less. In a perfect scenario they, too, will want to learn with you. Sharing what you learn about yourself and them can turn into another bonding experience, if that's desirable. The main goal is learning to move forward. However, it is also to remind yourself to not let any of what you decode spawn into resentment.

It's important for us to remember, they also had their own parents who conveyed onto them as well. The cycle keeps going. Except with you, because you are a badass and are about to break through the projected doubts!

You may be thinking, you don't have time to stop and reflect into your past each time a predicament comes up, but you do. Busy is another action and word all of us need to examine. In America, busy has become a word that has turned into a false synonym for important, responsible, productive, or all of the above simultaneously. Are you creating busyness just for the sake of it? Do you tell people you're busy when you're really not? Constantly busy is not healthy. I often hear conversations where one person is speaking to another, telling them they have been busy, and the reply they receive is, "Oh, that's good!" How do they know it's good? The person saying, they are busy could be internally crying for help because they feel overwhelmed, too busy, or like they have no time for themselves. The entire point of being human is to enjoy the time we have here, learn, and evolve. How is that supposed to happen if you are convinced that doing constant menial tasks is more important than self-knowledge? This busyness lifestyle has been taught to us at least since the industrial age. If we stay busy and "productive" for others, we forget about our own needs. How much time away from our families doing some type of labor that we placed on a false high priority list is enough? I certainly was guilty of this for far too many years. I thought if I wasn't at work, I should be doing something to improve my house, generate a side income — something, anything to keep myself as a high ranked "responsible, hard-working mother." Sometimes being too responsible is irresponsible. Having dishes in the sink does not take precedence over pool time with my kids.

How we process life doesn't just involve our current memories and lifetime. Internal, genetic programming can potentially include the surroundings and mother's lifestyle while in the womb, possibly even back generations through our DNA. If your ancestor lived through a tragic war, their PTSD can carry on through genetics into your thought process. If your mother had a stressful pregnancy, that stress could possibly still haunt you in adulthood. In the book *Super Genes,* Deepak Chopra and Rudolph Tanzi have gathered research around the topic of genetic effects. *Super Genes* states, "A Cambridge University geneticist in England, Ann Ferguson-Smith, published findings in the prestigious journal *Science* after testing the epigenetics implications of Dutch famine in mice. Heated criticism revolved around the key finding that a pregnant mother's diet has a long-lasting impact on the health of her offspring late into their lives. All mice were extremely underweight and prone to disease. The male mice who later went on to have children went on to have diabetes even though they consumed a normal diet." If we now know the diet of one mother can have effects on offspring for at minimum two generations, what about stress, fear, and anxiety? These factors are beyond our mental memory yet engraved in our genetic memory. Deepak and Rudolph go on to say, "Epigenetics suggest that our cells can in a sense 'remember' everything we have ever experienced. Old fears, wounds, traumatic events, and accidents litter the mind, roaming at will and distorting how we view the present." [iv]

While all of this sounds pretty scary, science is showing that we can also transform our DNA and guide it into bringing the positive traits to the forefront. Some of these traits our body does on its own. Some people are more immune to the common cold or, like me, immune to chickenpox, measles, or mumps. I was born immune to all of these, and before giving our children the fairly new chickenpox vaccine (not around when I was a kid), I asked our Nurse Practitioner if she would test our children for immunity as well. My daughter is the only one of three also born immune. Our genetics have intelligent memory, but they also have a cleverness in adaptability. In 2008, Dr. Dean Orish and Nobel laureate, Elizebeth Blackburn made a breakthrough, showing that lifestyle changes improve gene expression. One of the most looked at changes had to do with the gene telomerase. Supporting research has shown that increased telomerase, the enzyme that builds telomeres, might delay aging. The Ornish-Blackburn study discovered that telomerase did in fact increase in subjects following the positive lifestyle program Ornish recommends. The Chopra Center strengthened these findings by looking into the mental and spiritual components of a changed lifestyle.

If genes carry the memories of our ancestors and lifestyle change helps to activate particular memories, this means we can pull from our ancestor's brilliance, stamina, physical health, and resilience, as well as our own. The genetic makeup of each individual is unique; add sixteen years of trauma or love, and the genetics begin to change. Add more years, and there will be more change. If we consciously work through our negative experiences and trauma with self-knowledge and meditation, we take back control of what our DNA and subconscious mind bring to the stage. Imagine the shift this can create, not only for ourselves, but for future generations as well.

Some view our current society as angry, but what they mostly are is hurt without proper expression. How many times have you heard an adult tell a child to stop crying? Boys especially are made to believe that if they cry, they are "crying like a girl" or need to "toughen up." My favorite is "stop crying before I give you something to cry about." What the hell does that even mean? And why do so many parents continue to repeat it when we all hated that statement as a child?! This one small aspect of our childhood has transformed into a lot of confused adults. Too often we see those who do express sadness or fear as weak. They are told they will never make it in the business world or they will be taken advantage of in a relationship. Thoughts, such as these, are what come across our mind. In turn, we go out of our way to consciously and subconsciously suppress any real feelings, especially around others. I noticed a meme recently with thousands of likes and agreeing comments that said, "As a young woman you have to learn how to put your money and education before your emotions. That shit will leave you unfocused and broke." This is what we tell our young people, and although that was directed to women, it also applies to young men. I was that person, almost emotionless unless it was a movie or song. This was an unconscious way for me to release without having to connect it to my life. Of course, I loved people; I was a young mother, so I had learned deep love and emotions for my son, but crying rarely happened for me. When someone did something that I felt was un-loyal or hurtful, I showed anger. Anger is too often presented to us as a strength. It means we don't allow others to take advantage of us without giving them some sort of repercussion. In reality, when examined consciously, anger is frequently triggered by a hidden sadness. This is especially true when angry with those we love.

If we do as the meme I mentioned above and only focus on education and money, pretending nothing can cut us, then we will bleed on everything we touch. One day it will refuse to go unnoticed. This can take away all of that money you earned while being a hard-ass as well through emotional shopping, excessive drinking, drugs, or countless hours of therapy. Dealing with it in the moment creates much less turmoil and challenges us to try and sort it out. If someone has said to you that being emotional is weak, stop and ask, "Who the hell told you that? What does your life and happiness look like? Does it align with how you want to live?"

"Those who cannot remember the past are condemned to repeat it." This quote was said by George Santayana in the year 1905. It was slightly changed by Winston Churchill in a speech to the Houses of Commons when he said, "Those who fail to learn from history are condemned to repeat it." Your history teacher may have also used this quote to try and persuade you to study the facts presented to you in class, but it goes immensely deeper than what you learned in 8th grade social studies. To learn what the ancestors before us failed to see is more than the fall and rise of governments. It is the rise and fall of our household, careers, relationships, and personal contentment.

Have you ever noticed a symbol that seems to follow you or that has a particular appeal to you for no apparent reason at all? Symbols were used in ancient cultures to communicate and record. Some symbols have been around since the time of human's first use of tools to articulate how they felt and what was happening in that time period. They wanted future generations to feel the same connections. For me, it was the spiral. Long before I dove into the study of theology and cultures, I noticed the spiral and circles within circles everywhere I went. The book *Sacred Symbols* edited by Robert Adkinson states, "The circle and the centre. although most immediately associated with the religions of India and Tibet, the mandala, literally 'circle,' is one of the most potent symbols of humankind. Its circular form and concentric structure reflect the shape of the universe outside and the sense of perfection within. Concentration on its form and content is an aid to prayer and meditation, leading eventually to a complete ability to be at one with the world."[v] I don't believe in coincidences, and I also feel this was pure ancestral history poking me on the shoulder. To release the wars of yesterday, we must strive to understand the root, so that we may heal.

"Impossible is just a big word thrown around by small men who find it easier to live in the world they've been given than to explore the power they have to change it. Impossible is not a fact. It's an opinion. Impossible is not a declaration."

—MUHAMMAD ALI

CHAPTER 3

Transcending the Negative

Rising above the negativity that we face every single day can often feel impossible. Even throughout this book, I have mentioned several factors that could have jaded our subconscious mind. I know that many of you have faced much worse. Some have lived through circumstances that no living being should ever have to suffer through. If that is you, I salute you, encourage you, hold space for you, and cheer in your front row because I know you are more powerful than you have probably yet come to believe! It hurts in your heart, and your mind has impressions of haunting visions, but keep going. Don't give up on what the infinite possibilities of today, this week, this lifetime has in store for you and those you love. The one and only certainty in our world is change. You are not the same person as you were ten years ago. Your cells, skin, hair, thoughts, organs have all transformed into something new. It kind of makes us alchemist without any thought, right? Think about your hair. You don't have any of the same hairs as you did ten years ago, maybe even two weeks ago depending on how short you cut your hair. The body is constantly rejuvenating, rebuilding and repairing itself. This is all done without any thought on our part; it's just the wondrous nature and science of the human body. Now imagine what can happen when we apply the power of our mind. We have the ability to rebirth our happiness, thought process, and reactions in the same manner. The abilities that source gives us is pure potential for our visions to transpire.

You have the capacity to reprogram your subconscious mind. It has worked like a recorder your entire life, and it is what usually makes your decisions. This can be a good thing because it has taught you not to walk in front of a moving vehicle or get too close to the edge of a cliff. It can also lead you to make decisions that are not so good for you, detrimental to your desires and to your true dharma (life's purpose). We want to keep the positive and record over what no longer serves us. To do this will take some practice and patience. It will not happen overnight. You are not Cinderella. The following tools will provide daily activities and "rituals" that can be useful in this plan to reformulate the thinking development.

Use an hour by hour "Positivity Plan" with affirmations.

Daily, even hourly, positive affirmations stabilize the thoughts of the Now, keeping a steady flow of good intentions — and those intentions are what create outcomes. Hourly affirmation statements slowly become the quiet thoughts of your mind with little effort. Below is an hour-by-hour schedule of positive daily affirmations that will help keep you and your thoughts in a positive mindset, helping to avoid negative self-talk and limiting beliefs. If the times don't match your exact routine, use these ideas to create your own daily affirmation schedule.

5:30 a.m. – Before Your Feet Hit the Floor

- I am grateful.

- I am healthy.

- I am confident.

6:30 a.m. – After Your Morning Meditation

- My mouth is healthy (while brushing).

- I am beautiful/handsome. (No more putting yourself down while looking in the mirror!)

- My wardrobe says _____.

7:30 a.m. – On Your Way to Work

- I am always safe.

- I love my current situation.

- You can also pull motivating and powerful words from your music if you listen to music on your way to work.

8:30 a.m. – At Work

- I am surrounded by supportive peers and managers.

- My compensation exceeds my hours.

9:30 a.m. – Reset the Thoughts in Your Mind

- All that I do is a success.

- My work is completed on or before schedule.

10:30 a.m. – Mid-Morning Personal Affirmation Break

- I am in a loving relationship.

- My children are happy and safe.

11:30 a.m. – Pre-Lunch

- I will be the leader in the choice of my meal.

- My digestive fire is preparing for nutrition.

12:30 p.m. – Step Away From Your Work for a Relaxing Lunch

- I am thankful.

- This food is nutritious and healing.

- I eat at the perfect pace.

1:30 p.m. – Fight the Post-Lunch Lull

- I am full of life and energy.
- I focus my mind on productivity.

2:30 p.m. – Manifest Greatness

- I deserve success.
- Success comes with intent, not hours.

3:30 p.m. – Connect with Your True Self, as it Can Get Lost on the Job

- I am one with higher wisdom and awareness, immediately, now, eternally.
- All channels of my mind are open to receive from my higher thoughts.

4:30 p.m. – On Your Way Home

- I am always safe.
- I leave all work behind for the day.

5:30 p.m. – At Home

- I enjoy my family and friends.
- My home is peaceful and in order.
- My home reflects my energy of love and acceptance.

6:30 p.m. – At the Evening Meal

- I am thankful for all plants, animals, and workers who have participated in my meal.
- My body and mind are one with perfect health, now and eternally.

7:30 p.m. – Winding Down

- I am one with abundant prosperity and financial supply.

- I release all fear and worry.

8:30 p.m. – Evening Shower or Relaxation

- Clean is a high vibration.

- My body is balanced, young, and healthy.

- I am equal to the power of the entire universe.

9:30 p.m. – Check-In

- I am one with the perfect fulfilment of my life.

- I stay in the now.

10:30 p.m. – Last Affirmations of the Day

- As my transcendent higher self possesses my body, I accept all guidance to receive increased abundance.

- Happiness is me, and I am happiness.

As it may be hard to remember to do this on your own, especially at first, I suggest using your phone as an alarm. Since it takes 21 days to create a habit, try these hourly affirmations for three full weeks. Take notes about your feelings, outcomes, and thoughts, as this new way of thinking becomes part of your daily life and routine.

You do not need to believe these statements to speak them or think them. If you don't yet believe that you are peaceful, that's okay. That is what reprogramming and repetition is all about. Write it, practice it, and affirm it until you believe it! When you believe it and feel good about your own personal actions, dreams, beliefs, and relationships, the world and universe will follow your lead. When you set the intention of change, you will start to catch yourself when acting or speaking in a way that doesn't align with the new goal, that's great! No need to beat yourself up about allowing something to slip into the mind. The important factor is that now you are recognizing it. After recognition comes the change.

You probably noticed there was an allotted time that said, "after meditation." If you do not yet have a daily meditation practice, I deeply encourage you to add this into your routine as well. Meditation is good for literally everything, so it's no surprise that it will be helpful in retaining the positive and discarding the negative.

The most common statements people say to me when I mention meditation to them is, "I can't turn my mind off like that," "I don't have time," or "I pray." Meditating is not about turning your thoughts off. It is about observing them, which, in turn, helps to control them while out of meditation. Humans have 60,000-80,000 thoughts per day. Sometimes I think I have 150,000! If you don't have thoughts, you're probably dead. So, with that excuse out of the way, let's move on to the second excuse I hear the most: time. You have time. How much time do you spend on social media, watching TV, playing a video game, or better yet, complaining? Gotcha! You have it; now use it. You will also be pleasantly surprised with how much time will open up for you once you continue a mediation practice. Time is just a measurement. Something we utilize to let us know when to be where. It's a magnificent tool, but a terrible master. Just like the mind, we must take back our power, learn what the Creator gave us as tools, and stop allowing them to imprison us.

Third excuse eradicator. I commend you for praying and will cover more on the topic of praying a little later, but it's not meditation. Meditation is taking the time to control and observe thoughts, so that you can hear the Universe/Creator/God/Allah speak back to you. If praying is speaking, meditation is listening or at the very least maintenance on the airwaves. Our minds are bombarded with our own thoughts, plus the noise of the outside world almost 24/7. For those of you who sleep with a TV on and do not meditate, you may have hit the 24/7 marker. Dogs, kids, television, radio, videos on the phone, spouse, co-workers, someone is almost always trying to communicate with us. When do you give time and space for your instruction manual from the universe to download? You know that prayer you have been speaking on? Well, you can't hear the call when the lines are all occupied. I like to think of it like talking on our cellphones. If you speak with your phone and your receiving speaker is broken or you continue to allow call waiting to interrupt with that annoying beep … see where I'm going here?

Meditation practices come in bountiful variations. It's really about finding what works for you. When you first begin, you may gravitate to one form, and that may mold over time with more love for what you're doing and the results you are witnessing. A few options are:

- Guided Meditation
- Tibetan Singing Bowl
- Painting
- Coloring
- Sounds of Nature (preferably actually in nature)
- Watching Nature
- Listening to various chants or mantras
- Sitting in pure silence
- Repeating a mantra

I received my personal mantra while attending a Chopra Center retreat in Chicago. This is where I also met my friend and teacher, Davidji. At the time he was the Dean of the Chopra University but has now expanded and grown into his own educational system. I highly recommend you search his website davidji.com for easy, free guided meditations, especially if you're new to meditating. Guided meditations, in my opinion, are the easiest form of meditation with the most effective outcomes. It's literally a no brainer. You don't have to think about what your topic, music, or mantra will be; the guide has done all of the preface work for you… push play.

Easy peasy. Meditation alone is not a religious practice, yet all religions have some form of meditation, often in the form of mantras. In the book, *The Secrets of Meditation,* Davidji reminds us of this. He states, "Chanting the Catholic rosary, practicing Kabalistic hitbodebut meditation, praying one of the Buddhist Lam Rims, repeating Allah's name in Islamic dhikr, or the responsive reading of the Yoga Vasistha. All are repetitive and devotional practices giving glory to the divine."

YouTube is a great resource for listening to the singing bowls and chants. If you're not sure what type of chants to look up, maybe begin with the chakras. Each has their own unique sound or correlating vibration. From the base of the spine the chakras move up along the spine.

I Know   Crown

I See   Third Eye

I Speak   Throat

I Love   Heart

I Do   Solar Plexus

I Feel   Sacral

I am   Root

Name of Chakra - Location - Sound

1. Root - Base of spine - LAM

2. Sacral - Two inches below the belly button - VAM

3. Solar Plexus - Two inches above belly button - RAM

4. Heart - In center of chest - YAM

5. Throat - In the center of neck - HAM

6. Third Eye - Forehead center, just above eyebrows - SHAM

7. Crown - Just above the top of your head - OM, Silence, or AH

Now, let's move on to another easy trick you can do right now. Gather some scrap paper or sticky notes and a pen. Find some of your favorite quotes, perhaps some I have written in this book even. Then write them down to tape, stick, or tuck around your house, car, and office. Place them in areas where you can see them, but also hide some in books, a wallet, boxes, and the console of your car, for you to find later on. You may be surprised that just when you have forgotten about them or are having a rough day, *bam!* … the universe sends you into that compartment.

You probably noticed that throughout each chapter I ask a lot of questions. These are questions that only you can answer. No one can answer them for you as you have lived a unique life with your own perspectives. Some of the questions you may not yet know the REAL answer to, although you have a response. We all typically give a response to such deep questions based upon ways of thinking. If you are new to this level of self-knowledge you're only answering from where you are today. No worries, we all do it. Going back to the subconscious mind and the ego mind, the goal is to reach a level of personal consciousness that you not only recognize your own triggers, excuses, and bullshit answers, but you also allow the universe to flow the deeper answers into you. You may already have some of those answers on your own. If so, great but don't dismiss the fact that you may not have them all. A great way to arrive at the answers is asking the right questions.

If you are not coming to conclusions that make sense, begin to stir up more questions or transform the questions from another angle. I suggest starting this process with journaling. Divide your journal into sections with tabs. Use this outline to create categories and a starting point.

1. Repetitive Phrases

Write down the top five phrases you remember adults repeating when you were a child. These top phrases molded you in ways that you may not have yet explored. Ask yourself, which good traits came from them and which traits you would prefer to leave behind. For example: A parent who was in a war may tell their child to eat all of their food because there are starving children in the world. This is true, there are. I can't imagine what emotional pain a soldier endures from what they have seen and experienced, but this statement and forced action is not beneficial to anyone. Children who are made to eat all of their food could become overweight or produce suppressed feelings of guilt because they have food and others do not. I do believe children should be informed but maybe in a more beneficial manner, such as asking the child to put less on their plate, eat leftovers, or share with those who are in need. Do you find yourself repeating these same statements to your children, as well as whispers to yourself?

2. Word Association:

Make a list of these words. Next to each word write down the first word you think of after reading it.

- Work
- Meditation
- Love
- Money
- Anxiety
- Relationships
- Happiness
- Mistakes
- Family

Were the associated words and thoughts happy? If so, awesome! If not, elaborate in your journal on each word and how it made you feel.

3. Compare

Open your journal, so there is a fresh clean page on both the left and right side. Make a list of 10 things that describe success on the left. On the right side, draw a heart and write 10 things that you love inside the heart. Color and decorate the heart. Don't be afraid to make your journal a unique piece of art as you go. After you're all done with both sides, compare the two. If your ideas of success are not in alignment with what creates happiness and love, it may be time to reevaluate what success *REALLY* is.

4. Admit

> *"We cannot change anything unless we accept it."*
>
> —CARL JUNG

Write down all the things you need to admit to yourself. Behaviors you need to work on changing, hurt feelings you suppressed, etc. Reflecting back through the book at the various topics may be helpful here.

5. Dump and Detach

> *"Ultimately spiritual awareness unfolds when you're flexible, when you're spontaneous, when you're detached, when you're easy on yourself and others."*
>
> —DEEPAK CHOPRA

This quote is a great reminder that we cannot stay attached to old ideas and philosophies that don't provide room for spiritual and mental growth. Detach from that bad thing that happened, detach from the pain your carry, detach from that person you don't like.

The journaling process helps us actually take the time to thoroughly process what happened, analyze it, and let it go. I recently spent a week with the Tibetan Buddhist Monks of the Tashi Kyril Monastery. Almost anything negative that you ask them how to resolve, their answer (in short) will be to detach from it. Detach from what we have been groomed to view as important and love one another.

6. In the back of the journal, or a separate one altogether, write down your goals, dreams, plans, and affirmations that resonate with you. Also, leave a section for random epiphanies.

Handwriting is important. The way you write is unique to you. Someone else can try to copy it, but it will never be exactly the same. Have you ever noticed it even changes depending upon your mood? So write down all the future plans when you are in a good headspace. We "spell" our life with the letters that flow onto paper. This is why written words of intention are often called "a spell." Computers, phones, and all our gadgets are convenient, but they cannot replace journaling by hand.

7. You may want to consider burning some of the pages. If you feel you are comprehensively finished with a particular topic or memory and want to be all the way removed from it, burning it can help give us a visualization of that intention. I also suggest the same if you choose to write a letter to someone in your past that you have no intentions of giving it to. You wrote the letter for your own personal declaration not to dish-out to the other party.

"Deep within, you know that the only thing that is truly important is being in alignment with spirit."

—WAYNE DYER

CHAPTER 4

Alignment

Get into a habit of asking yourself, "Does this align with the life I am trying to create?" We are raised to eat a particular diet, for example. Our parents decided the cuisine, what the cabinets were filled with, and how often we ate at a restaurant, and that was all we knew. If you were raised in the south in the United States, you may have never tasted the food served daily in East India. Many of us walk through the grocery store, purchasing the same items that we recognize. We know we like them; we know how to prepare them. This is one reason obesity is a problem, more so than genetics. It's continuing on a path that our parents started, afraid to "waste" our money on vegetables that we don't know how to prepare or may not like. How much time we spend in the fresh produce section verses the frozen meal aisle is also preconditioned. It does take time and money to explore other options, but oh, what amazing outcomes we will find on that journey. Life is that same grocery store. Where your attention, time, and money are spent determines just how exciting life can be, *especially* attention.

You dream of travelling to exotic locations, but you have never been on a plane. The fear of the unknown stalls the adventure of a lifetime. Fear of physical harm can save our life, but it can also be our worst enemy. Tapping into your intuition is a useful tool in these situations. Go over the list of why you are afraid. More often than not when we are scared to participate

in something with a low probability of danger these thoughts are coming
from what we have seen, heard or been told. Statistics are useful when we
dream of experience, but fear holds us back.

I grew up in the concrete jungle of Cincinnati. Before there I lived in the
Appalachian Mountains and took two vacations my entire childhood. The
ocean was a foreign place to me. My first real experience with the ocean
I was a little nervous. The thoughts of sharks, their speed, and not being
familiar with the water in Freeport, Bahamas, all the scenarios ran across
my mind. Lucky for me I watched a lot of animal adventure shows. I knew
the probability was extremely low. I cannot imagine now, looking back on
this thrilling free trip to the Bahamas (which was also my first time in an
airplane at age 23), not absorbing all of that healing salt water. What would
have happened had I never stepped into the water? Would this have set a
path of repeated fear, had I not played in the ocean on that trip? Taking
a look at shark attacks, National Geographic reports, "You have a 1 in 63
chance of dying from the flu and a 1 in 3,700,000 chance of being killed
by a shark during your lifetime."[vi] Although, I personally know far more
people scared of a shark than the flu. Just the thought of being eaten alive
gives me the chills, but knowing the facts, I am not going to stop enjoying
the gift of salt water. When our soul calls us to an experience, we must
place our faith with the Creator and control the mind. This is also true for
our daily lives. Does your daily routine, job, home, and enthusiasm for life
align with what you desire? How much time and money do you spend on
escaping your reality versus making your reality something you don't want
an escape from? The average American spends $161 per month on cloth-
ing. That's a total of $1,700 per year!! How many of these purchases do you
suppose is unnecessary? How many of these shopping excursions do you
feel are emotional spending? There is nothing wrong with buying yourself
clothing, nothing at all. You deserve the very best! Spend well above the
$1,700 per year average if you wish, but ask yourself if it aligns with your
goals? Does it place you in a space of hardship? Do you shop and then beat
yourself up about spending extra money when you return home? Are you
making a purchase because you want to enjoy it or because it makes you
feel important? It is impossible for us to align with our true selves when
we allow "things" to own us. If the most expensive item in your closet gets

destroyed and it devastated you, it owns you. If you downgrade vehicles to save money and your first concern is what your coworkers, family and friends may think, it owns you. Things are here for us to experience, enjoy, and make life fun, not to define us or create a barrier between us and the life we are yearning to live. You are powerful! You can have it *ALL* but when learning the art of manifestation and subconscious control we must take each lesson and level gradually while advancing in our creative force. The daily practice will grow stronger with each passing day but having everything we want all at once, where is the fun in that? This is a game, play it!

The fear of alignment is real. If you're running from the realization of who you will become, you're not alone. For example, people often think becoming a spiritual person means they have to be nice all the time. This thought then leads to the fear of being perceived as weak or feeling as though they will have to put on a facade while around other spiritual people. Please! This side of life is not all rainbows and unicorns. You will get pissed off and sad and have various low moments; we all do. Often when the intuition flood gates open, we begin to see the truth of our upbringing, society, elite, and politics, making us become even more angry or scared than we were before. The path to enlightenment, discovering our authentic selves, and what it takes to live freely will uncover many variables of "truth." Regardless of which resources you are learning from, keep in mind that the fly does not see as the snake does. A fly has around four thousand lenses, and each lens performs independently. They also have a 360-degree view of the world, which is why it's so hard to sneak up on them, although their eyesight is actually not great. Some snake species, such as a boa, can see heat sources like infrared glasses. Think about not only the difference between the snake and fly, but also how they are both so different from us humans. All sights are seen from perspective. If we search for the perspectives and notice the daily reminders that we, the planet, and the universe are right on track, we all become magical healers through this holistic view of oneness. This reveals the capacity to know that although we are various organisms, we have a unifying power to help each other. Learning as much as we can is an amazing and fun adventure, but no outcome is set in stone, no matter how grim it may look or feel. I say this as a reminder that while searching for alignment many lessons may come your way that are not particularly fun.

I had a client who was dedicated to her pilgrimage of alignment and self-knowledge. She was an extremely intelligent woman with great success in business and community wellness. Every few weeks her manifestation practice took a hit. She would reach a plateau and become terrified of her own personal power. We met for a private session, and I expressed to her that she is worthy! The universal source is just waiting for her to accept that she can do even more greatness while in alignment with her happiness. By the end of our session, she said, "Wow! You are right. I have been told my entire life that wanting for myself is selfish. That humans are weak and fragile and must live a humble life. But like the saying goes, we cannot pour from an empty cup and not living in my dharma is draining all that I have!" For this woman in particular, she began her business more than twenty years prior. While it was successful, about eleven years in she realized her passion had transformed along the way. What once excited her now felt like torture. While giving up such an accomplishment may sound crazy to some, others see that true success is happiness, even if that means starting from the ground up … again.

The calibration of tuning in to what personal narrative we are striving to create takes patience and practice. Yoga and meditation are referred to as "a practice" because we never stop doing them. They are done with a goal of becoming just a little better each day. Evolution in any fashion must be practiced daily. If you go to the gym for a year straight and stop for five years, do you think your body will be in the same shape as when you worked out on a regular basis? Of course not. Not only do we need to practice daily to stay on course, but also because our thoughts, desires, and goals are ever changing. Just reading this book may have inspired you to change course from where you were when you started. When focused on alignment, think radio or TV frequency. Remember the rabbit ears that were once used to pick up a television station when we were kids? Each station required an antenna modification because each channel has its unique frequency. In terms of each goal objective, they, too, will be pursued by your frequency. In terms of bringing an experience into existence, like attracts like. This is one reason so many people feel that prayer doesn't work. They pray, think about what they desire, and are grateful for a few minutes each day, and then complain for the remaining fifteen to sixteen hours they are awake. If I told you for fifteen hours each day that I wanted one thing, but then told you the opposite for ten minutes each day, which one would you give me if you wanted to make me happy? The universal frequency is going to respond to what you are speaking and giving attention to the most. Manifesting almost anything has a gestation period. Thank goodness! Right?! Could you imagine the crazy things that would be popping in our house and car if not? The bad and good experiences just popping up around like popcorn from one location to another. You wouldn't want that; although you may say you want your creations to be instantaneous, it truly would be misery, and we wouldn't learn anything. This doesn't mean we never experience instant manifestations. I've personally had a few. While eating at a restaurant with a friend I said, "He didn't give us ketchup," and it appeared on the table. Of course, we both laughed, and that sparked our entire meal conversation around the topic.

Each day with each experience, we gather information — what we like, don't like, and how we want to live. What we want our legacy to be when we are gone. This is what genuinely aligning is all about. Pick up those pieces that make you feel good; leave the others behind. The more we do what we love, the more the universe serves it to us. Have you ever been around someone who just loves to cook? If you express to them how much you enjoy a particular dish, they are delighted to prepare it for you. The universe is no different, except the source has never ending access to ingredients.

Becoming spiritually aligned is becoming one with who we really are, what our soul mission to this earth was, what makes us feel whole. No one else on this planet can tell you what that means for you. It is also fluid. In various stages we too must be ready to change. The life purpose you had as a teen will look different than the life purpose you claim at sixty. Although your foundation and morals may be exactly the same, how we execute them may be through a different approach. What takes up the top three slots of the priority list will probably look like apples and oranges in comparison. I have witnessed many around this time in life start to feel regret for not following a passion earlier, but maybe, it wasn't even a passion then. Rarely does someone have the same passion out of high school as they do above thirty. Maybe now is the time to start whatever currently makes your soul feel good. Even if you allowed a dream to take a back seat, aligning now is okay, too.

We pray for jobs, money, a "picturesque" relationship, or what we have been led to believe was the best life possible on this earth, later discovering we didn't want any of it. Stress, disease, and fatigue manifest from living such a lie. We try to convince ourselves, it's just the way it is here on this particular rock that floats through space, as a human, as an adult ... but is it? When in the depth of these thoughts, I think we have probably all said, "There has to be more to life than this." Does it take a knock on the head to realize that we we're living outside of our spiritual alignment? Carrying on through the seeds of ideas someone else planted.

Although we each have our unique way to serve others and ourselves, I believe a few traits hold true at the core for all of us. Our most basic and genuine birthmarks are love, play, and unity. When we convey these mannerisms in all actions, the universe adjusts our experiences accordingly.

Alignment with our higher self is to step outside of the ego. Allow intuition to guide in the steps needed to heal, love, and achieve. When this becomes our goal, all other objectives fall into the path, and needs are met more effectively. Before we can do this adequately, we must first understand what the ego is. The ego is the thought that we are the labels we have not only placed on ourselves but that we adopted from how others described us. Humans become the job title, tax bracket, neighborhood, bank account, car, and popularity they adapt to and accept as "themselves." This is why so many get fired from a job they've had for years and feel they have nothing to live for anymore. They condensed their entire existence into a title or attachment to this particular success. We are not separate from each other or Creator, yet we base our entire life structures around believing we are. Yes, I am a separate human than you, but in the higher realm, the spiritual realm, the true meaning of all of this we are doing here comes to light: I am you, you are me, we are one. When connected to this, the individual that we call us can be free from the chains the ego holds us too. In some cases, one may insert the word humble here. I do not like the word humble. I feel there are already too many people thinking less of themselves and others, but I understand why this word is used. I would like to pause here to give you a deeper look into the word humble and its various definitions from The American Heritage Idioms Dictionary.

1. Not proud or arrogant; modest;

2. Having a feeling of insignificance, inferiority, subservience, etc.;

3. Low in rank, importance, status, quality, etc.; lowly;

4. Courteously respectful[vii]

While number four, courteously respectful, is fine, take a look at the other three. Are these things you would tell your child, best friend, or mother to think and speak about themselves? While being arrogant is never a good look and certainly something we want to avoid, feeling insignificant and of low importance is unhealthy and will manifest outwardly into a poverty mindset and life. Feelings of low importance can potentially transmute into life threatening depression, stress, anxiety, and low self-esteem. If you would like to take this little side project a step further, go online, plug humble into the thesaurus and scroll down the page. I think we can use more appropriate terminology to lift ourselves and others up. Maybe, we can use words such as gentle, kind, polite, divine, equality aligned, loving. Full circle back to listening to our higher self, finding that higher purpose, I would like to give you an excerpt from *You'll See It When You Believe It* by Dr Wayne Dyer. He says, "The clearer I became, the less negative and judgmental, the more I began to treat my physical self in healthier ways. As I allowed my purpose to find me, I began to feel happier and more in harmony with myself. Ultimately it was as if I forgot about myself and tuned in automatically to my strong sense of mission and purpose."[viii]

"This is a time of monumental shift, from the male dominance of human consciousness back to a balanced relationship between masculine and feminine."

—MARIANNE WILLIAMSON

CHAPTER 5

Man in His Image

For thousands of years we have lived in a patriarchal society. Many feminine things have been belittled and demonized. Whether these traits came from a woman or a man, they were weak and underneath the stronger masculine traits. After identifying these traits as weaknesses for so long, it made some of us attempt to suffocate our feminine emotions and not speak on intuitive visions. We were told we would never make it in the real world if others see us cry or we made any decisions based on empathy. I was personally guilty of this. Although I had female friends, I was quick to say, "Most of my friends are men" or "I get along better with men." Did I? Or in truth was I just learning how to be more masculine? Perhaps even absorbing the masculine energy, so I could later transform it into a protective, aggressive frequency when I felt threatened or wanted to prove I was worthy of success? I think the latter is the role I was playing. This lesson in particular was probably my longest-lived role. It's easy to become something that isn't our true self when we think it's what we need to survive. We tell ourselves we are just becoming our true self because it feels good to become "powerful." However, it is not your authentic power. It feels good as a young woman to not only survive in a patriarchal system but thrive. This would be true if it were reversed as well. It is all any of us living has ever known. Not just us but generations before us, transplanted into our genetics. The majority of our grandmothers were submissive to their husband, some overlooking infidelity or mental and physical abuse, and all because they didn't feel they had other options. In our current stage of evolution, a phoenix has risen! The feminine in all creatures, be it human or Mother Nature, is showing the external world that she has had quite enough!

Now, like a pissed off mother, we must still be delicate. As we as individuals and a human collective manifest our way into a masculine/feminine balance, loving each side equally is of utmost importance. If we go too far to the "women rule the world" mentality, we will just throw ourselves into another few thousand years of imbalance and inequality in the opposite direction.

We are all male and female. Being mindful of this in all we do will help us maintain the utilization of both traits. Remembering that without a beautiful dance between the two within us, the scale is tipped. The more we allow it to tip, the more we can rest assured chaos will occur. People of today have a preconception that individuals expressing themselves as the opposite gender, preferring not to be identified by specific gender, or practicing homosexuality are on some sort of mainstream "takeover." These individuals will point fingers of blame at media, music, and social circles. Media and music are typically expressions of the times, not the other way around. We can look back at art from any era and see that the artist was depicting what was going on around them and how it made them feel.

Using external, visual elements, the world shows an internal masculine or feminine expression that has been a part of fashion and individual articulation for thousands of years. Even within a patriarchal system these forms of style were, more often than not, accepted if you include our entire human timeline of information. Masculine and feminine attire are also a matter of perspective and opinion. "She wears the pants in the family." This is a clear expression that pants were equated with "the head of the house." Now, jump back in time to the Biblical era, for example, to when men wore robes. Today, this tradition has not changed in Arab countries where men wear a thobe, regardless of social or political stature. In East India the long male top is called a kurta, often coming to or below the knee. While pants are also worn under these long garments, often men of the Western Civilizations still have a hard time not computing that as feminine or "a dress."

Ironically, they have no harsh words for Jesus who would have dressed the same or very similar to what the culture still is today in these parts of the world.

Have you ever noticed how many of us refer to an animal that we don't know as "he"? How we say "he" more often than "she" when referring to a hypothetical professional in a story when we don't know the sex of the person? Even though we want equality, we continue to speak about certain professions as if we already know the sex. Doctors, lawyers, plumbers, car mechanics are often referred to as men. Nurses, restaurants servers, and hotel housekeeping, more often than not, are referenced as women in regular conversation. There are approximately ten to twelve thousand female plumbers in the United States. Do you feel there would be more if we spoke of them from a gender-neutral perspective? I often wonder how many children begin to think about their career choices based upon the vocabulary of the adults they spend time around.

The books of our past often use the term "man" when in actuality what they meant was mankind or humankind. The label of man separated humans from animals, spirits, gods, or Creator. This expression eliminated the need to break down each gender or age group. You can imagine while writing thousands of words on papyrus that reducing man, woman, child, boy, and girl down to one term would be a preferred method for the author. This is especially true when the message is for the entire human race. To further accommodate the patriarchy, some used these terms as manipulation tools to further keep women from learning about many important women of history.

Most importantly, we see this kind of thinking in religious books. Many of the most well-known spiritual leaders in history were male. Does this mean there were less female spiritual masters in our ancient past? I, for one, highly doubt it. The Gnostic Bible has shown us that Mary Magdalene was a teacher alongside Jesus, who also wrote about these teachings. Mary Magdalene even had her own book. This book was called The Gospel of Mary. What a difference for the female view around the world and Christianity that would've made. But even in the Gnostic Bible, Mary had a hard time.

I would like to share with you a couple of excerpts from the Gnostic Bible. In The Gospel of Thomas when Yeshua (Jesus) was gathered with a group of men and Mary, Shimon Kifa said to them, "Miryam (Mary Magdalene) should leave us. Females are not worthy of life." Yeshua replied, "Look, I shall guide her to make her male, so she too may become a living spirit resembling you males. For every female who makes herself male will enter the kingdom of heaven."[ix] This is extremely interesting to me. Was Yeshua talking about our internal balance of masculine and feminine? Was he letting Shimon know that her male side could be activated, and he planned to guide her in doing so? Was he implying that this made them equal? This would also be true for males who can welcome and balance their feminine aspects. He continues on to say, "When you make the two into one, and when you make the inner like the outer and the outer like the inner and the upper like the lower, and when you make male and female into one so that the male will not be male nor female be female, when you make eyes in the place of an eye, a hand in the place of a hand, a foot in the place of a foot, an image in place of an image, then you enter the kingdom of heaven."[x]

The Gnostic Papyrus collection is dated between the first and second century. This set of papyrus scriptures were accidentally found in Upper Egypt close to the town of Nag Hammadi by a man digging for soil in 1945. This man was a Muslim Camel Driver and didn't have a lot of money. The collection was divided among several drivers, some sold on the black market, and it took years to gather them all back up again. By the mid- to late-sixties, scholars now had the full collection of books to study and date. These sacred texts were believed to be destroyed when the Christians were fighting to define orthodoxy. Once found, we have to ask ourselves why the King James Version was not revised with these texts included, giving the public the option to replace their current Bible with this new profound information. These texts are filled with quotes by Yeshua. Is it because they did not want us to know that Mary Magdalene had her own book?

It doesn't really matter if you were raised in a religion or not. We all hear that the "perfect" beings are male. God is always referred to as "Him." Jesus, his perfect son, is another male. Even the most well-known spiritual leaders and teachers from our current time and past, also mostly men.

Buddha, Prophet Muhammad, Dala Lama, Pope, Martin Luther King, Louis Farrakhan, Billy Graham, Sadhguru. I could go on, but I think we see where I'm going with this. There were very few women to inspire other women within the lineup of spiritual teachers from our global history. This is certainly changing but has nonetheless had an impact on our world. There were and still are many that believe a woman should not speak or teach in the church. Sometimes women are told to do as their husband says, told that he is head of the house, the list goes on. While this concept is certainly found in the Holy Bible and Quran, it reaches other religions and even non-religious people as well. My parents, for example, did not go to church, but because my mom was raised in church, she spent her entire marriage to my dad believing that he was, "head of household," "boss," "in charge of decisions," etc. You do remember what I told you about my dad, right? This is our leader? I couldn't understand how she had this viewpoint. Why had this become so embedded into her subconscious? Why did a woman who did not go to church get so stuck in this rule? Yet, she didn't believe that Creator would want her to have better in life? Or, even more importantly, that Creator would take care of her if she left? These rules often override our better judgment. This not only leaves us in positions of scorn and negligence from others, but it also builds self-melancholy. If you're one of the few who didn't grow up hearing others say such things, you may think this thought process is antiquated, but it's still very present. I observe women of the community quickly change their personal opinions or politics to appease their husbands, despite how they personally feel. They truly believe that what their male spouse says is the way and she should follow. This also holds true with raising children, what to or not to spend money on, etc. This internal belief that regardless of personal intuition or what the heart or mind says, a woman must stay compliant to their husbands is detrimental. This does damage to not only her emotional and physical wellbeing, but also to any children involved. Do we want our children to see marriage as a partnership, both people important with valid opinions, or as one ruler over everyone else?

In spite of this patriarchal gloom from our past, a revision is here. Women, men, boys, and girls are shifting the frequency in favor of balance. Each gender is in the advanced stages of learning about our separate traits. Society is learning how the masculine and feminine energies both thrive within us as individuals to assemble a whole being.

Creator, as an energy source, must surely vibrate on a masculine and feminine frequency. How else would something be so great in balance, understanding, and creating male and female rhythm? Some even say that women were created from Adam, not God itself. While that may be fine for some and what the latest translation of the Bible states, I find it odd that the human female is the only female stated not to be a direct creation from God. Do views and perspective of this change once we observe the billions of animals, plants, and microorganisms from a male and female perspective? If we attempt to think of Creator outside of a human perspective, does nature balance both male and female? As I mentioned earlier, we all have both swirling around inside of us. Accepting that, nurturing each one for their uniqueness, results in healing and the desire to understand one another.

My husband was a stay-at-home father from the time our two youngest were born until they were around eight and nine years old. When I told others this, the most popular response from men was, "Wow, you've got a good one." Would they have given that same response if it were me at home and my husband telling them the same thing? I don't believe so. While yes, my husband was and still is "a good one," that is not really what that sarcastic response meant. Generally, I could tell their response was sarcastic by their tone. With others, their continued conversation and jabs at my husband's masculinity made it obvious. Interestingly, the number one reply from women was, "What? You need to make him get a job!" Yep! I'm not talking about just a few women here. Almost all women that I told had some version of that remark, not all of course. But too many women are still just as quick as men to believe the man's job is to work outside of the house while the women stay at home, if there is going to be one at home at all. What if the woman can make or is making more money or can work less hours and still provide enough to have a parent (in this case a dad) stay home? Is there not more value in one parent raising the kids than there is in spatting over which one is doing it?

I also encounter those that tend to think that stay-at-home moms or dads are spoiled or less valuable because they are not bringing in income. I've personally been on both sides of the coin. I had my oldest son at sixteen years old. From that point on my goal was to have a parent raising my children as much as humanly possible. I felt it was important that at least Mom or Dad was the one nurturing and implementing our values. I quickly found out that few shared those views, that being in the home was often perceived as a weak feminine role. In 2018 moms.com took a poll from twenty men to see what their thoughts were on stay-at-home moms. Below I will share seven of their answers with you.

1. "Although my wife is a stay-at-home mom with two kids, deep down I wish she worked."[xi]

2. "I believe I have a biased opinion in that my mother worked, and I employ many working mothers. Working mothers tend to have a broader understanding of choosing priorities and sacrificing fun-to-do things. They also seem to have a better appreciation for the value of hard-earned income. That's not to say that stay-at-home moms don't appreciate these things, but in my experience working moms appreciate them more."[xii]

3. "My wife is a stay-at-home mom, and I do think her job is harder than mine in that she works incredibly long hours. But it's also a low-skilled job, similar to cleaning houses or doing laundry, and due the laws of supply and demand, I do not think she deserves half my salary if we ever get a divorce!"[xiii]

4. "Only when I tried to get a job after being a 'mom' for 28 years, I was treated entry level! Lots of job counselors kept telling me how 'my skills were transferable,' but in reality, nothing I did for 28 years counted for anything in the job interview, whether given by man or women … So, to me, the question is not 'what do men think of women who stay home?' but 'what does society think of people who stay home?' And nobody, neither men nor women, respects the stay-at-home parent when in a business setting. In the mall, everyone loves it, but in an office, nope!"[xiv]

5. "I could never be with someone who is okay with not being able to provide for themselves. Being a mother is one of the easiest and most common things in the entire history of the human race."[xv]

6. "I think financially relying on a spouse or SO is a terrible idea, so I'd say I'm against SAHM. The reason is that in my opinion, both parties should be financially independent to avoid external reasons for staying together. If a woman has earned $0 in years, then how would she support herself without a man?"[xvi]

7. "Nothing wrong with being a stay-at-home mom. But, I'm a bit old-fashioned; I don't really buy that taking care of one kid (your own kid, no less) is by itself equivalent to a full-time job. You have to be doing a lot of things that make a single-income household livable."[xvii]

There were a few more not-so-encouraging comments, but on the flip side, about half were not only encouraging, but also spoke as a true partner in parenting and life. Once again, we are moving forward. This provides even more opportunity to question our thoughts and reactions when these topics arise in society.

Whether you're a mom or you just have a mom, you can see that the role of motherhood, including nurturing, teaching, and guiding our future, doesn't get the full respect it deserves.

Our son loves to show me YouTube videos. He recently shared one with me where women on the street were being interviewed during election time. A considerable number of women still believed that a woman should not be president because of her "hormones." Is this to say men never react from a testosterone imbalance or they do not allow emotion and ego to sometimes drive decisions? Are there roles that you feel are specifically for a man or a woman? Do these thoughts paralyze growth within your goals or household?

The patriarchal system has been just as damaging to the men on this planet as women, possibly more. In a system based upon relinquishing so many feminine gifts, men also suffer and have been damaged. My oldest son was a theatre kid all through high school and still as a grown man, loves to be on stage. There were times when I would speak about an upcoming play to a male who didn't know him and sometimes they would ask me if my son is gay or make what they perceived to be a gay joke. If he were gay, of course I would have no problem with that, but he isn't. To attempt to help them see why it was incorrect to jump to this conclusion, I would remind them that many of the most "masculine" actors on the big screen also started in theatre. This is just one example of how men who are just doing what they love have been victim to the patriarchal mindset. I'm currently writing this while all of the world is on COVID-19 quarantine. Two memes I have noticed several times on social media are:

- Posted by some women: "I bet you wish you would've got you a man that can hunt and build a house."

- Posted by some men: "many of you guys are mad that you didn't get you a woman that can cook?"

This is interesting to me considering data from 2018 shows that 77.6% of restaurant and hotel chefs are men.

As I mentioned previously, I grew up in a home where my mom did everything. I told you one side of the programming that this ingrained into my subconscious. In a previous chapter I shared with you the hatefulness I misdirected toward my husband, but what about with other people? Absolutely! This thought process created a temper in general when the topic presented itself as well as judgment. I have an aunt who always said she had to be home to cook for her husband at a particular time of day. I respect her, and it was really none of my business, but it did, for a time period, make my view of her different. While I was not around her often as a young child, the judgmental time period that I am speaking of was in my late teens and early twenties. I wanted to hang out with her. In my mind, we were going to have a good time, whatever it was I was asking her to go do. Now, as someone who has deeply analyzed previous thought processes, I see that they were still equal. He left the house daily to drive an hour to work while she did have a job, though the majority of her work was performed at home. Of course, she should be the one cooking. As a partnership, she is the one within the home. My dad not participating in our family as a team player had various effects on my thoughts. This is just one small aspect of how broadly our perspectives are altered by what we view as barely a glimpse of our full story.

The patriarchy system says that almost all emotions (outside of anger) are for women. How often have you heard an adult say to a young boy to stop crying "like a girl"? From this tender age he now begins to suppress his emotions in fear of not gaining the approval of the people around him. The adults have now stripped him of his masculinity for shedding tears. This is not just something a man says to a boy. I have heard countless mothers say the above statement. Why would a woman tell her son not to cry like her or her daughters? Because she, too, has heard this statement so often over her life that now it's just being repeated. She, too, wants to be accepted by the male circle as someone who raises her son the way men said it should be done. So often these remarks are just repeated, not consciously thought through. In these moments we have an opportunity to stay silent rather than speak. Ask questions before we affirm how another person should or should not act. To tell a boy he is crying like a girl is just one small example of how the patriarchy has and can harm everyone in the room. Let's pretend for a moment that a mother, father, daughter, and the son are all together when this is said. Subconsciously breaking each one down into their own personal fight or flight response. Each one having their internal turmoil and conversations. If the father is not someone who cries, he will feel like he is viewed as the strongest in the room. But after hearing such a statement will he now be more likely to hold back emotional or physical pain? The daughter may now feel like the weakest link. No one else in the room wants to cry like her, but at least she has a pass to do so. Will this too create an internalization of pain, so that these statements are not said anymore? The mother while feeling empathy for the children may also be concerned with how others may bully the children. Does she view the husband as weak if he comes to a breaking point with tears? Do these opinions harm the relationship and their open lines of communication in fear of judgment? There are so many subconscious scenarios that could be talked about here. Most of them would be resolved if we just encourage others to observe their feelings and cry when they feel like their soul needs a good cleansing.

Men who are emotional, nurturing, and kind are often viewed as weak by both men and women. To be taken seriously as a partner, friend, or parent, a man often hides his authentic feelings. This can lead to drug and alcohol abuse, disease brought on by self-hate, and explosions of rage. I have had many male clients in these scenarios. A man's best defense against the world's opinion of his kind nature might be to destroy this part of his ego. Not necessarily an easy task when first starting out, but it gets easier with practice. In the Bhagavad-Gita, Krishna says, "For one whose mind is unbridled, self-realization is difficult work. But he whose mind is controlled and who strives by appropriate means is assured of success. That is my opinion."[xviii] To get started in releasing ego for all genders, try the following;

- Release the need for others to like a false version of you.

- Spend time enjoying your own company.

- Practice gratitude for who you are.

- Think about what the word "respect" really means to you.

- Ask yourself and examine how judgment can actually upset you verses how you were told to deal with it.

Many of our ancestors created a cycle that we are now trying to find harmony with. Observing our feelings in each and every moment and listening to intuition, we can overcome our fight or flight responses. Periodically, we may make the mistake of rallying behind a female that was in the wrong or prosecuting a pure-hearted man because we are quick to jump to conclusions. We may mistakenly see a situation as sexist based upon our subconscious imprint. After several cycles and generations of these fights, we are sometimes reacting in defense, fight or flight, and survival modes. Regardless of what you call it, the shift is here. Now, more than ever, it is time for us to analyze situations and stories before reacting or overreacting.

We can also look back at the not-so distant past. A couple hundred years ago some of the Native Americans were living like many cultures around the world, in a matriarchal society. Being of Melungeon/mixed heritage myself this includes Cherokee and Shawnee. The United States is so mixed, so diverse, like many areas around the globe, to the point where, now, many of us genetically "remember" a time when we were equal. This adds to the situation, and so the fight that started with the feminist movement was for various reasons, inevitable. In 1757, it was recorded that a male Cherokee leader, named Attakullakulla, questioned the European men sent by Great Britain, "Where are your women?" The history and laws of the Cherokee show that their women enjoyed a level of autonomy that their Euro-American counterparts could have only dreamed about. The traditional culture and formal laws of the Cherokee respected women and did not subjugate them to men. The Cherokee culture and laws offered all women power over many forms of property, the ability to sell property on their own accord, absolute control over their children, the ability to divorce, and political power. In stark contrast, the contemporary eighteenth and early nineteenth century Euro-American woman would not have enjoyed any of these rights during marriage, as law expressly forbade them. Cherokee women's legal rights were embedded deeply in their culture and, seemingly, were immutable. In 1827, the Cherokee people had been convinced to create their own constitution, which stated, "No person shall be eligible to a seat in the General Council, but a free Cherokee male citizen, who shall have attained to the age of twenty-five years."[xix] By 1831 the Trail of Tears had begun, and Native Tribes were not allowed to legally practice their spirituality openly again until the year 1978.

I would like to also share with you a letter sent to Benjamin Franklin from a Cherokee woman of the Chota area in 1787. This entire letter does not pertain to my message to you, other than her strong leadership, of course. I could've just pulled a couple sentences, but I thought you may enjoy the letter as much as I did/do.

Brother,

8th Sept., 1787.

I am in hopes my Brothers and the Beloved men near the water side will heare from me. This day I filled the pipes that they smoaked in piece, and I am in hopes the smoake has Reached up to the skies above. I here send you a piece of the same Tobacco, and am in hopes you and your Beloved men will smoake it in Friendship — and I am glad in my heart that I am the mother of men that will smoak it in piece.

I am in hopes if you Rightly consider it that woman is the mother of All — and that woman Does not pull Children out of Trees or Stumps nor out of old Logs, but out of their Bodies, so that they ought to mind what a woman says, and look upon her as a mother — and I have Taken the privelage to Speak to you as my own Children, and the same as if you had sucked my Breast — and I am in hopes you have a beloved woman amongst you who will help to put her Children Right if they do wrong, as I shall do the same — the great men have all promised to Keep the path clear and straight, as my Children shall Keep the path clear and white so that the Messengers shall go and come in safety Between us — the old people is never done Talking to their Children — which makes me say so much as I do. The Talk you sent to me was to talk to my Children, which I have done this day, and they all liked my Talk well, which I am in hopes you will heare from me Every now and then that I keep my Children in piece — tho' I am a woman giving you this Talk, I am in hopes that you and all the Beloved men in Congress will pay particular Attention to it, as I am Delivering it to you from the Bottom of my heart, that they will Lay this on the white stool in Congress, wishing them all well and success in all their under-takings — I hold fast the good Talk I Received from you my Brother, and thanks you kindly for your good Talks, and your presents, and the kind usage you gave to my son. From

Katteuha,
The Beloved woman of Chota.[xx]

Inspiring to say the least! There are many questions that surround these stories that we can not only pull inspiration from, but utilize to question our own personal thought processes and fires of ambition.

There are a few exercises we can do to lift up the masculine and feminine sides of our brain. As I mentioned above, we each have masculine and feminine traits. Our true power lies in nurturing both aspects: accepting them as who we are and learning how to utilize their strengths.

When you would like to nurture your masculine side, you may look at doing an exercise that involves the following.

- Word/Verbal Language

- Math

- Facts

- Logic

- Realistic

To nurture our feminine side, the below activities will be a good tool.

- Visualization

- Intuition

- Holistic Thinking

- Arts

- Feelings

Clearly, we need both sides to optimize balance. One is not better than the other. Being of one specific gender does not equate to choosing a lifestyle or career path that aligns with one side or the other. Hopefully, we have covered that. You may be a woman who is an outstanding mathematician or a man that is an incredible artist. What it does mean is that we must consciously make an effort not to criticize either side of our sexual traits, use each trait as needed, and consciously provide the attention that all of our aspects crave. Even the traits that may not be our strongest are there at our disposal. A mindful practice of building each side will help us in our daily lives and understanding others.

For masculine exercises, give these a go:

- If constructing isn't really your thing, maybe take a class on building something small. Local hardware stores often offer classes for small projects. Habitat for Humanity is another outlet ready to train and thankful you are there. This builds on our math skills to pump up the male thinking.

- Test your strength ability with some weight lifting or, my personal favorite, carrying as many grocery bags as possible from the car.

- Do something competitive. Play video games, try an outdoor sport, or participate in a cook off. Almost any activity that you enjoy can be turned into a competition.

For the feminine side of you, try these exercises:

- Perhaps you could focus on being more holistic in thought. The word "holistic" means to look at any situation as a whole. In health, this thought process is to treat all aspects of human health in mind, body, and soul versus just the area of discomfort. In photography, it is to look at the entire picture instead of zoning in on just one color or object. Think of ways throughout your day that you can bring in a more holistic approach. Looking at the full completed version — how one act, thought, or process affects the other.

- Welcome emotions that you previously would have ignored. Why do you want to cry at the toilet paper commercial? Is there something that you've been holding in all day? Crying is washing our soul of hurt feelings or frustration. When we allow ourselves to release, we can start fresh the next day. Suppressed and repressed emotions have their own dangers, outside of our opinions of weakness, which we discussed in chapter one.

These are just a few examples of what we can do to nurture our beautiful makeup, the cosmic dance of masculine and feminine. Create some of your own and let's build the bridge internally as it will reflect externally.

"What we see depends mainly on what we look for."

—JOHN LUBBOCK

CHAPTER 6

Accountability

Stop making excuses for the negative actions or attitudes that you revert back to, despite knowing that they are not serving you. You've lived with yourself for a long time now. You know most of the traits of which I speak. Although some words and priorities of the past work themselves into your brain without much thought, you are still aware of some of your unfavorable traits. I know, I know … It's just who you are, right? I've been there, said that, gotten the T-shirt. Like me for who I am, or don't. Which is great. We do want to show our authentic self to the world and attract those that love us based upon our true self. But how many of those "just me" traits are no longer serving you? Some may have never served you.

Don't confuse authenticity as rationalization for being an asshole or rude. It can't be used as a reason to not improve and evolve in new directions. I was speaking to a dear friend just recently who had taken her stepmom on vacation to celebrate her birthday/retirement. She said, "My mom is a control freak. If anyone else would've talked to me the way she did, I would've had some harsh words for them." Being in a state of conscious awareness, she realized that she, too, treats people the way her stepmom was treating her. By the end of the trip she was saying to herself, "That is something I need to change about myself because that is annoying!"

Look at how people just blame their negative actions on their zodiac sign. For example, I'm a Gemini — one moment I may be happy and nice, while 3.5 seconds later I am in full dragon mode and completely imbalanced. As my teacher and friend, Davidji, says, "Scorching an entire village." Does this mean that because I'm a pitta/Gemini that it's okay for everyone around me to endure my wrath? For me to say, "I'm a Gemini, it's just how we are" is immature and lazy. It doesn't improve my life or the life of anyone around me.

Not to go too deep into the zodiac, but imagine we came to this earth to work on the negative aspects of our birth sign and karmic past while utilizing the positive traits to help us do so. Evolution is part of what this life is all about. Rather than just accepting actions and thoughts that you know could be improved, use all of the indisputably good aspects of the zodiac to transform who you are. Create new traits that serve you more effectively, with less stress and anxiety. Instead of anger, ask yourself why you are angry, rather than exploding on another person. When we question these personality traits, we are forced to see ourselves. We start the road to admitting that maybe we do have the temper of our father and the neglect of our grandmother. It may be a little weird for you and those around you at first. Your friends and family are going to notice the small changes. Share your adventure with them. They can help you by being honest in what they see as their favorite qualities in you and how they have seen you take the negative too far.

One lady came to me asking how she can manifest less drama in her life. I asked her how she typically reacts when there is a low frequency situation. After much time and many questions, I discovered that when someone was upset with her, she just avoided them as much as possible, not wanting to deal with the matter. This kind of avoidance in turn only makes the situation build into resentment from the other people, including close family members. This just keeps creating more drama with people that you are going to continue to see. As much as you may want Suzie in cubical eight to go away, she is still there. The fear of drama alone will create more drama. She knew she always avoided any hint of confrontation. Knowing this had not yet solved anything. The thought of trying something different, like a calm conversation with honesty, just never really crossed her mind. Coming out of a verbally and physically abusive relationship had almost completely shut her down when it came to taking up for her opinions and thoughts. It is not always drama, although a difference of opinion can feel like it may go that direction.

These intense fears are like praying for what we don't want. The universe speaks in frequency, so continually projecting these vibrations outward, is certain to boomerang back.

When it comes to accountability, think of what you would say to a child. Throughout my life I have noticed that adults are quick to demand accountability from children, or adult friends even, but are slow to demand it from themselves. Perhaps this is because our ego has such a determined drive to stay alive, to feel important. We allow the voice of the ego to convince us it's the other person's fault, it's the result of our circumstances, or we don't want to be "burned" yet again.

Let's talk about the ego for a moment. The word and meaning of ego can be interpreted in a couple different ways. It can mean your confidence level, which is a wonderful trait to have. Keep the confidence, ditch the "I" attitude or the "Id" as Sigmund Freud referred to it in his Ego Personality Theory. To find more on the Freud research you can find it in the book, *The Ego and the Id*. You can have high levels of confidence without everything or anything being about you, actually it shows more confidence. We've all been to a party or get together where one person just has to be the constant center of attention. When this attention begins to dissipate, they may do something outlandish, loud, or just off the wall to once again get all eyes on them. This is often perceived as confident or the life of the party, while others see this as a parallel act to a child whose parents never spend quality time with them. It's the same with the various parts of the ego. The basic level of ego (Id) wants to survive, be seen and heard, and have instant gratification by all means necessary. The median ego is the part that wants to keep the ego happy but also understands that being too selfish will land you alone. The next level is the superego, the higher consciousness ego that has self-love and respect with full awareness that none of that has to do with instant gratification, selfishness, or shaming another. The superego takes pride and gains more confidence with acceptance and working toward betterment within and without.

As you go through this work, you may experience a growing awareness of ownership in which you realize when you have treated others and yourself unfairly. Work on releasing those moments, rather than feeling guilt. Don't get caught up in "would've, should've, could've" in your reflections. You will say and think it, but then release afterwards. It's not like you were truly aware of what you were doing. Sometimes we get stuck in our own personal fight or flight mode; that's okay. It happens to all of us to some degree. Watch it roll by like a trailer to a movie on fast forward. If there are areas that deserve extra attention, work through those without giving them control. Again, take ownership, take the power away from what happened, and make it different today. If a situation stands out consider writing yourself, another person, or perhaps both, a letter of apology. If the other person is no longer in your life; write the letter then burn it as I suggested in a previous chapter. You have done your part to bring back the balance and healing. If they are in your life, tell them how you feel.

If we look at some of the political, racial, and religious tension going on around the world in the present day, many just want one group or another to take accountability. Even if they personally had nothing to do with the history of the situation. I recently attended a convocation at Berea College where the keynote speaker was Vance Blacksmith, a Lakota elder who teaches at Oglala Lakota College on the Pine Ridge Reservation in South Dakota. He spoke about white men coming to America and how the Lakota young people are still angry, saying things like, "We should kill them." Their anger is understandable, but thoughts of murder are poison to themselves and others. The tragedy, genocide, and destruction that happened and is still happening has not been publicly acknowledged or accounted for by the American Government. This keeps resentment going, generation after generation. Blacksmith also said that his answer to this anger is, "No, that is not our way. We wait for their spirit to be ready to learn. Then we teach them because they too are Lakota people." (Although I have talked a lot about gender, nationality, and heritage because it does play such a major role in our conditioned thinking, we are all one. I do see a day that we will heal and move past all of these divisional labels.) In these types of deep-rooted traumatic occurrences, it's important that we take a step back and look at it from outside of our emotions. Authentically, there are several interior levels of emotions that can and will affect our temperament when certain subjects arise. Going down the rabbit hole of our true emotions can help us build upon what will help us all to heal in a way that is productive. What were the dynamics that not only affected our psyche, but also our ability to love others and our children? What happens if we don't end the cycle? Many states have now taken Columbus Day off the calendar as a holiday and replaced it with a Native American acknowledgement. This is the type of accountability that we are all looking for in these types of situations. Accountability begins to open up the lines of communication. This platform is true, whether there are multiple people/parties involved or we are just taking accountability for ourselves. Let's pretend for a moment that you have set a goal to get into shape. Weeks and months go by, and you have hardly worked out at all. You're mad at every circumstance you can think of, and the more the days pass, the more emotional about it you become. You start resenting the kids because you don't have a sitter to go to the gym, but even if you did, you've now spent your gym membership on a babysitter and can't afford to pay to workout monthly. Your "baby daddy" doesn't help; your mom is always on vacation … This snowball could roll into an avalanche, or you can stop yourself and become accountable for your actions. Once this consciousness shifts, now you begin to workout at home and create activities for movement with the kids, and the new higher frequency opens the doors for more financial abundance that can support a membership now too! We will not get there by holding onto anger or expressing anger toward others or ourselves. Love, compassion, and patience are the way. Learning to transform that blaming disposition into something useful will benefit generations to come and make solid improvements.

When we acknowledge that something did, in fact, happen that should have never happened and we as an individual/community/country stand in solidarity to prevent it from happening in our future, healing has begun.

How many people do you hold resentment toward when in reality you truly just want an apology? Some sort of admittance of what they did to hurt you, so you can move forward. So you know it wasn't just you blowing things out of proportion when your feelings were hurt. Perhaps also to build back some kind of relationship. Accountability often shows that we not only own our mistake, but we want to do better in the future. Keep in mind, with that said, although that is helpful you don't need that to heal, and you may not always get it. Once we are aware that this is what we're really longing for, then we can also release that drive.

Once accountability has been acknowledged and the conversations have been had about the incident, you may choose to tell the other person about their wonderful qualities, too. We all have beautiful traits. Sometimes those traits get overlooked because they are not the attention getting, hurtful attributes of a person.

There is a story about the Babemba tribe that has been floating around America since the 1970s. This story began with the book *The First Four Minutes* by Leonard Zunin, who says this tribe has a unique approach to punishment. You may have heard Dr. Wayne Dyer speak on this story as well. In the Babemba tribe, if a person has done something unethical, irresponsible, or against tribe rules, they have a ritual to rehabilitate the person that can last hours or even days. The person who committed the "crime" stands in the middle of a circle that is made up of the other tribe members. They dance around their loved one and individually tell the accused all of the great qualities they admire about them, stories they remember of this person being kind, making someone laugh, being a light for the tribe. All ages, even little children take part in this ceremony. Could you imagine how that would reactivate your personal power to be all those great things once more and release what negative thing that recently occurred?

Some say this story is false and has no factual evidence but honestly, I don't care either way. The story has been talked about for at least forty-five years in the United States. It has inspired every person who has heard it, I'm sure. It makes us reflect upon on our thoughts and actions toward people who have hurt our feeling or harmed us physically or mentally. Accountability is important, but it's more important that we take a look at our own accountability rather than trying to force it on the ones we haven't forgiven. Once we forgive that individual, the story has a new perspective. Forgiveness is for ourselves, our personal healing. This does not mean we have to be around the person ever again, but we can take a look at understanding how they perhaps stepped outside of their best selves and wish healing for them as well.

We often want others to hold us accountable when we have a new chapter of ourselves to improve. Sometimes individuals depend so much on others holding them accountable, they don't show up or follow through with activities to improve their own wellbeing. Why do so many people crave a gym, yoga, meditation partner? As humans we are social creatures. When we stop to think about it, we really do spend a lot of our lives with others. It is normal to sometimes feel out of place or lonely when we first begin something all alone.

While it is fabulous to have our friends around to participate in achieving our goal, we won't always have someone else to lean on. With this said, there are a ton of you self-motivators out there as well! More people are successfully working from home than ever before. This would not work for anyone who is not determined to get projects done without a scheduled day or a boss over their shoulders. Companies are recognizing that generally when you give people the freedom to work on their terms, they actually get more done while being happier.

Financial gain may be a little more of a motivator than let's say, cleaning out the walk-in closet or cooking dinner verses ordering delivery. What are some projects or self-improvements you have been putting off? Is it time to hold yourself as much liable for the things you dislike as the ones you like? For example, I was once addicted to soda, and I wanted to greatly reduce this intake, so I started purchasing other drinks as a replacement. After some time, I wanted to also reduce the pre-made drinks and make my own tea, smoothies, etc. If I had pre-made drinks in the house, I would reach for one of every time. After a while I noticed I didn't even like the taste of a soda as much as I previously did but was still choosing this over making a pot of tea. Anyone who knows me will tell you, I've always been a self-motivator to the extreme. My personal realization with the soda and tea scenario was that while I am motivated, sometimes I chose to let the little things slide if they interfered with what else I wanted to be doing. Finding a solution usually takes less time than listing off all of the excuses we tell ourselves.

Practicing holding ourselves accountable is extremely important. Each day set a goal that you are obligating yourself to accomplish by the end of the day. A simple, easy task that can be incorporated into your normal routine without stress. Use this list to help get you started.

Just for today I will …

- Compliment at least one stranger.

- Drink the amount of water my body needs.

- Be mindful.

- Listen to the people who are speaking to me by being fully present in the moment.

- Tell someone outside of my household that I love them.

- Meditate for five minutes.

- Not say one negative thing about myself.

- Cook something healthy.

- Say a silent prayer for at least one person that I pass by today.

- Be authentic with myself and others.

After you practice the list alone, select one to play with your friends; hold each other accountable and share your stories. Sharing life is enjoyable, but we don't want to rely on it. I have heard several people say, "I used to workout but _____ stopped going with me." If we depend on other people to always be by our side, we may miss out on many things we want to accomplish. During our teen years, it's generally easy to find a friend to go out to eat, hit the gym, or walk on the beach with. As responsibilities grow, what we enjoy changes along with our schedules and who we want to spend our free time with.

Keep in mind that accountability starts with you. How can we expect others to take accountability for their hurtfulness and unjust acts if we can't even take accountability for what we want in life? You are a wonderful leader. If you don't feel like a leader outside of yourself, I hope you can at least agree that you are the leader of you. Your actions, goals, and determinations must begin and end with you and you alone. Help from others is just icing on the cake. Take ownership, kick ass, and inspire others to do the same just by observing your actions.

"What seems to us as bitter trials are often blessings in disguise for which we are later, in the fullness of time and understanding, very grateful for!"

—OSCAR WILDE

CHAPTER 7

Don't Shoot Your Own Foot

The journey of life is to be enjoyed, but it's often viewed as stressful. Sometimes, it's because we can't see on the other side of the door. Where we are has become our stability, even when we are actively manifesting something more, something better. When the blessings come, our doubts can push them aside.

If you were offered a new, phenomenal job by someone who saw potential in you, but it is something you have never officially done and is completely outside of your qualifications, do you take it? Too often this answer is no. Validation and credibility are lacking in the person who so badly wants to move forward but can't grasp the vision of worthiness. They feel they don't know enough to accept such a wonderful opportunity. Richard Branson says, "If somebody offers you an amazing opportunity but you are not sure you can do it, say yes — then learn how to do it later!"[xxi] I would have to agree! You can always learn as you go. Did you really know all of the technicalities of the job you do now when you started? We could spend years in classrooms to learn a particular job and still not have a clear understanding until we are in the thick of it. If we have a passion for what we do and the desire to be great, we should be striving to learn more all the time anyway.

How often have you prayed for peace? Peace of mind is one of the most important aspects of this human life. For some it seems harder to come by than a billion dollars! Neighbors fighting, work gossip, road rage, family that just never seems to be happy for you, friends who feel relevant based on the drama they can attract. You wanted those endless negative situations to go away, yet when certain people stop contacting you, you chase them. You cannot figure out what you could have possibly done to upset them. Why don't they stop by the house anymore or pick up your calls? They always have plans when you invite them to dinner; is it you? Remember what you ask for before getting upset when your routines change. It can be a painful experience when we break up with a friend. Do we use this word friend with too much lifelong engagement attached to it? Friendship, love, romantic partners, every so often we come across someone and just tell ourselves they will be in our life forever. We have imprinted this on our vision of the future so deeply that we never stopped to consider that we may drift apart or we may have never been that close in the first place. With eight to fourteen-hour workdays, how often do we become "friends" with someone out of convenience and circumstance? Once that person leaves that place of employment, the friendship drifts apart, and before long it's been years since you spoke. We can love people in the space we are allotted with them, but if we tell ourselves a story of how it will play out, we may become more hurt when it is time for the next chapter.

Humans are strange … all of us. At some point in our lives we will pray, day in and day out, for a particular situation, experience, or relationship. Then, when it presents itself, we will unconsciously push it away. Our subconscious mind may not be able to process that there is such goodness available to us. Too often we've convinced ourselves that the life we were living is It, that's the peak! Anything else is for "other people" or maybe we feel we haven't worked to the capacity which we think it would require. We must stop begging the Universe to make it so, just so we can wrangle with it upon arrival.

In the book, *Boethius - The Consolations of Philosophy*, Boethius is serving a prison sentence awaiting execution. Philosophy comes to him as a vision of a woman. She says to him, "And if you see a man who has done what he wanted, you will hardly doubt that he had the power to do it, will you?"[xxii]

Rarely do we question the blessings of others as much as our own. The "grass is greener" mentality with a twist, if you will. Why do we think the other person has achieved their platform easier than us when we are struggling? Why do we feel they have less stressors if they are happy? We take ownership of our obstacles, so they can be the excuse in our minds that are verbally expressed to others when we want to give up or turn down growth. It is easier to pout, criticize, or devalue ourselves and others, instead of seeking to improve and repair. Repair takes work and so does growth. We know if we step out of our routine to accept this new blessing, it will require maintaining. This holds true for a romantic relationship, career, new house, less drama, or higher tax bracket. Philosophy, as the woman, says to Boethius "…men's power or ability is to be judged by what they can do, and their weakness by what they can't do."[xxiii] We judge ourselves and stop our personal power based upon fear, lack of validation, accreditation, or past failures. To own our power, it takes a will to move past all of these hurdles. Taking note in our lessons and trusting the Universe to place us where we are supposed to be is also a form of power. What does the word 'Power' mean to you? Stop here for a moment to write down what comes to mind in correlation to this word.

This is one of those words with a plethora of meanings. If I say to you, "I want power," you can take that sentence and compute it to mean almost anything that aligns with your current viewpoint. Let's take a look at what Webster's Dictionary says on the word Power.

When you first click onto the word power online you notice across the top a category section that reads:

All - Politics - Law - Military - Religion - Physics - Sport - Electrical - Mathematics

Taking a look at the categories, how many never crossed your mind with my above affirmation?

Moving on to the many definitions:

1. The right or means to command or control others[xxiv]

Synonyms for *power*

arm, authority, clutch, command, control, death grip, dominion, grip, hold, mastery, reign, rein(s), sway

2. The ability to exert effort for the accomplishment of a task.[xxv]

Synonyms for *power*

energy, firepower, force, horsepower, might, muscle, potence, potency, puissance, sinew, strength, vigor

3. A natural ability of the mind or body.[xxvi]

Synonyms for *power*

faculty

4. Something with a usable capacity for doing work.[xxvii]

Synonyms for *power*

energy, fuel

These are four very different definitions with synonyms to back up those variables. Each word we hear hits us differently based upon our past experiences, our current state of mind, and what belief(s) others have shared with us about the word. For example, if I tell you I want power and your only thought of power is definition number one, you may think I'm a horrible person. If you align more with definition number two, you may give me encouragement for the stamina to keep pursuing regardless of the exhausting obstacles I face.

In the book *Sacred Powers*, the author, Davidji, says, "…when we convince ourselves that what we want to happen won't and what we don't want to happen will, then we become a victim of our dumbed-down, constricted versions of ourselves."[xxviii] How do we get out from under that version of ourselves?

- Being aware that they exist.

- Recognizing the variables in which we feed these thoughts.

- Defining the categories we are most likely to approach with our constricted selves.

- Praising ourselves for the areas where we bring our best selves and apply openness.

- Read quotes or books that inspire and remind you of your true potential.

- Enjoy the experiences that each day brings.

The *Bhagavad Gita - As It Is* states in the translation of the sacred text, "In the minds of those who are too attached to sense enjoyment and material opulence, and who are bewildered by such things, the resolute determination for devotional services to the Supreme does not take place."[xxix] The purport expands on this to follow up with, Samadhi means fixed mind. When the mind is fixed for understanding of Self, it is said to be in Samadhi, yet Samadhi is never possible for those more interested in material gains, for those are temporary things. While material items are enjoyable, priorities accordingly, self-knowledge can never be stolen.

Notes

Notes

Notes

Notes

Notes

Notes

Notes

Notes

A Few of My Favorite Ancient Quotes

"*You can search throughout the entire universe for someone who is more deserving of your love and affection than you are yourself, and that person is not to be found anywhere. You yourself, as much as anybody in the entire universe, deserve your love and affection.*"

—GAUTAMA BUDDHA

"*Jesus answered them, Is it not written in your law, I said, 'Ye are gods?'*"

—JOHN 10:34 OF THE KING JAMES BIBLE

"*I have said, Ye are gods; and all of you are children of the most high.*"

—PSALM 82:6 OF THE KING JAMES BIBLE

"*Most powerful is he who has himself in his own power.*"

—SENECA, DIED 65 CE IN ROME

"*The unexamined life is not worth living.*"

—SOCRATES, LIVED IN ATHENS CIRCA 450 BCE

Bibliography

Adkinson, Robert. *Sacred Symbols: Peoples, Religions, Mysteries.* London: Thames & Hudson, 2009.

Ammer, Christine. "Humble." Essay. In *The American Heritage Dictionary of Idioms.* Boston, MA: Houghton Mifflin Harcourt, 2013.

"Anger Management: Your Questions Answered." Mayo Clinic. Mayo Foundation for Medical Education and Research, March 5, 2020. https://www.mayoclinic.org/healthy-lifestyle/adult-health/in-depth/anger-management/art-20048149.

Baer, Drake. "14 Quotes from Ancient Thinkers That Show They Figured Life out 2,000 Years Ago." Business Insider. Business Insider, May 11, 2020. https://www.businessinsider.com/wise-quotes-from-ancient-philosophers-2016-4.

Bawden, Amanda. "'Our Share of Land': The Cherokee Nation, the Federal Government and the Citizenship Status of the Freedpeople, 1866-1907." "Our Share of Land": The Cherokee Nation, the Federal Government and the Citizenship Status of the Freedpeople, 1866-1907 - UEA Digital Repository, June 29, 2017. https://ueaeprints.uea.ac.uk/id/eprint/63983/.

Benson, Jennifer. "Are You Repressing Your Emotions?" health enews, May 19, 2020. https://www.ahchealthenews.com/2019/02/15/are-you-repressing-your-emotions-2/.

Carver, Melissa. "Daily Affirmations: Your Hour-by-Hour Positivity Plan." The Chopra Center, March 7, 2019. https://chopra.com/articles/daily-affirmations-your-hour-by-hour-positivity-plan.

Carver, Melissa. "How to Balance Your Female and Male Energy." The Chopra Center, November 4, 2019. https://chopra.com/articles/how-to-balance-your-female-and-male-energy.

"Chefs & Head Cooks." Data USA, 2020. https://datausa.io/profile/soc/chefs-head-cooks.

Chen, Robert F, Arthur Eisenkraft, David Fortus, Joseph Krajcik, Knut Neumann, Jeffrey Nordine, and Allison Scheff. "Robert F. Chen." SpringerLink, 2020. http://link.springer.com/10.1007/978-3-319-05017-1.

Chopra, Deepak. *Super Genes: Unlock the Astonishing Power of Your Dna for Optimum Health and Well-Being.* Place of publication not identified: Harmony Crown, 2017.

"CONSTITUTION OF THE CHEROKEE NATION." Digital History, 2019. http://www.digitalhistory.uh.edu/active_learning/explorations/indian_removal/cherokee_constitution.cfm.

Curreri, Jason Alexander. "Lost in Transition: The Waning of Cherokee Women 's Independence from 1808-1832." Seton Hall University , May 1, 2013. Lost in Transition: The Waning of Cherokee Women 's Independence from 1808-1832.

Davidji. *Secrets of Meditation: a Practical Guide to Inner Peace and Personal Transformation*, 153-53. Carlsbad, CA: Hay House, Inc., 2017.

Dave, and Joy. "All-Natural Product." Work with Dave and Joy, June 24, 2019. https://workwithdaveandjoy.com/tag/all-natural-product/.

Dutton, Judy. "What Dads Really Think of Moms Who Stay Home With the Kids." CafeMom, February 26, 2015. http://thestir.cafemom.com/being_a_mom/181762/what_dads_really_think_of.

Dyer, Wayne W. *You'll See It When You Believe It.* London: Arrow, 2005.

"Franklin Papers." Packard Humanities Institute: The Papers of Benjamin Franklin, n.d. https://franklinpapers.org/framedVolumes.jsp.

"Gautama Buddha Quotes About Self Esteem: A-Z Quotes." AZ Quotes, n.d. https://www.azquotes.com/author/37842-Gautama_Buddha/tag/self-esteem.

Gear, Spencer D. "Bible Bigotry from an Arrogant Skeptic." Truth Challenge, February 16, 2016. http://spencer.gear.dyndns.org/category/bible/page/5/.

Gleason, Meg. "Nat Geo WILD: What Are the Odds? Some Surprising Shark Attack Stats." National Geographic Society Newsroom, December 14, 2017. https://blog.nationalgeographic.org/2011/11/22/nat-geo-wild-what-are-the-odds-some-surprising-shark-attack-stats/.

"Laws of the Cherokee Nation." Common Law, April 15, 2019. http://www.commonlaw.com/home/legal-history-and-philosophy/laws-of-the-cherokee-nation.

Louis, Adrian C, and John Hoppenthaler. "Adrian C. Louis - Poetry." ConnotationPress.com, September 2012. https://www.connotationpress.com/hoppenthaler-s-congeries/2012/july-2012/1479-adrian-clouis- poetry.

Moore, Lisa, Joanna Brooks, and Caroline Wiggington. *Transatlantic Feminisms in the Age of Revolutions*. Oxford: Oxford University Press, 2012.

"Power Synonyms, Power Antonyms." Merriam-Webster. Merriam-Webster, 2020. https://www.merriam-webster.com/thesaurus/power.

Prabhupada, A.C. Bhaktivedanta Swami. *Bhagavad-Gita As It Is*, 1972. http://bharata.info/books/Bhagavad-Gita%20As%20It%20Is.pdf.

Roer, Carrie. "Humility." In the sweet sunshine, December 7, 2008. http://carrieinthesweetsunshine.blogspot.com/2008/12/humility.html.

Stapleton, Alice. "Top 5 Tips For Starting Your Own Coaching Business: Blog," 2020. https://www.alicestapleton.com/blog/top-5-tips-for-starting-your-own-coaching-business.

The English Bible. King James Version. New York: Norton, 2012.

"The Gnostic Apostle Thomas: Chapter 2." The Gnostic Society Library, 1997. http://gnosis.org/thomasbook/ch24.html.

"The Gnostic Apostle Thomas: Chapter 24." The Gnostic Society Library, 1997. http://gnosis.org/thomasbook/ch24.html.

"Turistòleg." 2015, December 18, 2015. https://turistoleg.blogspot.com/2015/.

Watts, V. E., and Thomas Browne. Essay. In *Boethius the Consolation of Philosophy*, 119–19. Baltimore, MD: Penguin classics, 1969.

Index

Endnotes

i "Anger Management: Your Questions Answered," Mayo Clinic (Mayo Foundation for Medical Education and Research, March 5, 2020), https://www.mayoclinic.org/healthy-lifestyle/adult-health/in-depth/anger-management/art-20048149.

ii Jennifer Benson, "Are You Repressing Your Emotions?," health enews, May 19, 2020, https://www.ahchealthenews.com/2019/02/15/are-you-repressing-your-emotions-2/.

iii Ibid.

iv Deepak Chopra, *Super Genes: Unlock the Astonishing Power of Your Dna for Optimum Health and Well-Being* (Place of publication not identified: Harmony Crown, 2017).

v Robert Adkinson, *Sacred Symbols: Peoples, Religions, Mysteries* (London: Thames & Hudson, 2009).

vi Meg Gleason, "Nat Geo WILD: What Are the Odds? Some Surprising Shark Attack Stats," National Geographic Society Newsroom, December 14, 2017, https://blog.nationalgeographic.org/2011/11/22/nat-geo-wild-what-are-the-odds-some-surprising-shark-attack-stats/.

vii Christine Ammer, "Humble," in *The American Heritage Dictionary of Idioms* (Boston, MA: Houghton Mifflin Harcourt, 2013).

viii Wayne W. Dyer, *You'll See It When You Believe It* (London: Arrow, 2005).

ix "The Gnostic Apostle Thomas: Chapter 2." The Gnostic Society Library, 1997. http://gnosis.org/thomasbook/ch24.html.

x "The Gnostic Apostle Thomas: Chapter 24," The Gnostic Society Library, 1997, http://gnosis.org/thomasbook/ch24.html.

xi Judy Dutton, "What Dads Really Think of Moms Who Stay Home With the Kids," CafeMom, February 26, 2015, http://thestir.cafemom.com/being_a_mom/181762/what_dads_really_think_of.

xii Ibid.

xiii Ibid.

xiv Ibid.

xv Ibid.

xvi Ibid.

xvii Ibid.

xviii A.C. Bhaktivedanta Swami Prabhupada, *Bhagavad-Gita As It Is*, 1972, http://bharata.info/books/Bhagavad-Gita%20As%20It%20Is.pdf.

xix "Laws of the Cherokee Nation," Common Law, April 15, 2019, http://www.commonlaw.com/home/legal-history-and-philosophy/laws-of-the-cherokee-nation.

xx Lisa Moore, Joanna Brooks, and Caroline Wiggington, *Transatlantic Feminisms in the Age of Revolutions* (Oxford: Oxford University Press, 2012).

xxi Alice Stapleton, "Top 5 Tips For Starting Your Own Coaching Business: Blog," 2020, https://www.alicestapleton.com/blog/top-5-tips-for-starting-your-own-coaching-business.

xxii V. E. Watts and Thomas Browne, in *Boethius the Consolation of Philosophy* (Baltimore, MD: Penguin classics, 1969), pp. 119-119.

xxiii A.C. Bhaktivedanta Swami Prabhupada, *Bhagavad-Gita As It Is*, 1972, http://bharata.info/books/Bhagavad-Gita%20As%20It%20Is.pdf.

xxiv "Power Synonyms, Power Antonyms," Merriam-Webster (Merriam-Webster, 2020), https://www.merriam-webster.com/thesaurus/power.

xxv Ibid.

xxvi Ibid.

xxvii Ibid.

xxviii Davidji. *Secrets of Meditation: a Practical Guide to Inner Peace and Personal Transformation*, 153-53. Davidji, *Secrets of Meditation: a Practical Guide to Inner Peace and Personal Transformation* (Carlsbad, CA: Hay House, Inc., 2017).

xxix A.C. Bhaktivedanta Swami Prabhupada, *Bhagavad-Gita As It Is*, 1972, http://bharata.info/books/Bhagavad-Gita%20As%20It%20Is.pdf.

About the Author

Dr. Melissa Carver began as a contributing writer with the Chopra Center in 2014. This experience sparked a much deeper love of reaching others through the written word.

She has taught hundreds of courses around the US and has been a prominent keynote speaker at conventions and retreats alike.

Melissa is also the founder of the nonprofit organization, Mindset Junkies. This organization focuses on funding programs and scholarships for low income families to learn the power of mindfulness, primarily the families of those in drug or alcohol rehabilitation or US Veterans.

Outside of her PhD in Philosophy, Dr. Carver is certified as an Ayurvedic Chopra Instructor, Nirvana Flow Specialist, and has continued post graduate education in Counseling Psychology.

Her intention is to help others break out of the perspectives that bind them to negative actions, becoming the best versions of themselves, just a little... day by day.

Find out more at drmelissacarver.com - Sign up for her free newsletter here as well.

https://www.instagram.com/dr_melissa_carver

https://twitter.com/carver_dr

https://www.facebook.com/drmelissacarver/